The Rational Investor

How to Beat Wall Street, Build Passive Wealth and Stop Worrying About Money

Ben Le Fort

ISBN: 9781777963569

Dedication

To Trish, my love. Thank you for your patience as you endured countless hours of me talking about investing and index funds. It was not for nothing.

Is This Book For You?

"*All models are wrong, but some are useful.*"

That quote from George E. P. Box is one of my favorite quotes of all time and is instructive on what you should expect from reading this book. This book draws on the most influential research papers from the most brilliant minds in finance to help you answer a simple but important question.

"*What is the rational way to invest your money?*"

The papers, data, and models referenced in this book are in a sense, "wrong" because any model falls short of explaining exactly how the world works all of the time. We don't know what will happen in the future. All we can do is use the best available information to guide our expectations and decisions.

All models are wrong, but some are useful.

The aim of this book is to provide the best available evidence to help you maximize investment returns without taking unnecessary risks or paying too much in investment fees.

You should always be skeptical of any information presented to you. Be especially skeptical of people who don't show their work.

If I can guarantee you one thing, it's this: I'll show you my work. The reference page of this book will point you to some of the most ground-breaking research in the field of finance.

If you have already made up your mind about investing and would be unwilling to change your opinion if presented with credible evidence, this book is not for you. As the ancient philosopher, Epictetus said, "*It is impossible for a man to learn what he thinks he already knows.*"

However, if you have an open mind, and are willing to listen to evidence that might contradict your worldview then this is the investing book you have been waiting for.

Setting the table…

You've probably heard of passive income, but you may not have heard of the term passive wealth before.

Passive wealth is when you have an investment strategy that is so simple and requires so little of your attention that your wealth begins multiplying when you're not paying attention.

In fact, it works best if you literally pay it zero attention.

My investment strategy is so simple that if I decided to go live in a cave for the next 10 years, my portfolio would likely outperform most of the top fund managers on Wall Street.

This might sound like some investment guru bull$hit artist who is trying to sell you their investment course in a YouTube ad, but that couldn't be further from the truth. I am talking about investing in low-cost, passively-managed index funds.

Index funds are referred to as "passive investments" because they passively track the performance of the entire stock market rather than actively trying to pick stocks that will outperform.

If that sounds boring, that's because it is.

The world's most famous stock market index is the S&P 500 index which tracks the performance of the 505 largest public companies in the U.S. No, that is not a typo; it's called the S&P 500 even though it has 505 companies. I guess the S&P 505 doesn't have the same ring to it.

As simple and boring as index investing is, it's also highly profitable. Consider, for example, that S&P 500 index funds have outperformed 83% of actively-managed investment funds over the past decade at the time I write this. So, when I said I could go live in a cave for 10-years and still outperform the majority of Wall Street managers that is not hyperbole but a matter of fact.

In this book, I will present the mountain of academic and industry research that suggests most people should buy a handful of low-cost index funds and hold onto them until they reach retirement age. Economic researchers have answered some of the toughest questions in investing, but there's a big problem; economists are terrible at communicating simple ideas. Anyone who has ever read a peer-reviewed economic paper knows that economists write for other economists—which is to say long, boring and overly technical.

While I would never claim to be on the same intellectual level as the researchers I will cite in this book, I have enough training to be able to translate their work from "economic speak" into something both comprehensible and actionable.

But first, let's spend a few minutes discussing why you bought this book. On the surface, you likely bought it because you want to become a better investor. But, why does it matter if you are a good investor? Because you understand that the more your money works for you, the more opportunities and freedom you'll enjoy throughout your life.

Why passive wealth is the ultimate financial goal

"Money doesn't buy happiness" is often said by people with lots of money and have never known what it's like to live without enough money.

Of course, money buys happiness. But, not because it allows us to buy fancy toys and live in a big house. Money buys what all of us desire: freedom and a sense of control over our lives.

The brilliant behavioral economist Daniel Kahneman published a paper in 2010 which found that emotional well-being or happiness does not increase as a result of making more money beyond a $75,000 threshold.[1]

This $75,000 threshold was thought of as a happiness plateau, and most people accepted it as gospel because, well, who are we to argue with Daniel Kahneman?

But a more recent paper by Matthew Killingsworth, a senior fellow at Penn's Wharton School, finds that more money does increase happiness even beyond the $75,000 threshold.[2]

Killingsworth studied 33,000 individuals providing real-time feedback on their well-being an app. Killingsworth asked participants to fill out short surveys at random times during the day. Killingsworth calls this type of real-time feedback "experience sampling". The app collected 1.7 million responses to questions like "how do you feel right now" or "how satisfied are you with life?"

The idea is that by collecting enough snapshots of people's lives over time, you begin to build a clearer picture of what makes them happy.

1 Kahneman, D., & Deaton, A. (2010). High income improves evaluation of life but not emotional well-being. *Proceedings of the National Academy of Sciences*, 107(38), 16489–16493. https://doi.org/10.1073/pnas.1011492107

2 Killingsworth, M. A. (2021). Experienced well-being rises with income, even above $75,000 per year. *Proceedings of the National Academy of Sciences*, 118(4), e2016976118. https://doi.org/10.1073/pnas.2016976118

Unsurprisingly, the major finding was that more money makes you happier, even above the $75,000 per year threshold.

To be fair, the marginal contribution of money to happiness decreases over time. An extra $10,000 means a lot more to someone making $30,000 than it does to someone making $300,000. But the person making $300,000 is still happier if you hand them $10,000.

Killingsworth's hypothesis for why more money continues to make us happier; it's not about buying more things. It's about buying more control.

As Killingsworth told Penn Today.[3]

> *"When you have more money, you have more choices about how to live your life.*
>
> *People living paycheck to paycheck who lose their job might need to take the first available job to stay afloat, even if it's one they dislike.*
>
> *People with a financial cushion can wait for one that's a better fit. Across decisions big and small, having more money gives a person more choices and a greater sense of autonomy."*

The more money we have, the more often we can say "no" to things that make us unhappy. Once we have enough wealth, we gain enough control over our lives to choose to only engage in activities that fulfill us and make us happy.

It's called "FU money".

---

3 *Money matters to happiness—perhaps more than previously thought.* (2021, January 18). Penn Today. https://penntoday.upenn.edu/news/money-matters-to-happiness-perhaps-more-than-previously-thought

If you want happiness, you need control. If you want control, you need to start accumulating FU money. If you want FU money, you want to maximize the total net returns of the money you invest. So, if you want more control and thus more happiness, investing surplus money in index funds and building passive wealth is a pretty great place to start.

This book explores a mountain of evidence that suggests that investing in low-cost, passively managed index funds is the key to maximizing your total net returns.

Table of Contents

Part 1:
The Investment of Choice to Build Passive Wealth

Chapter 1:
Detecting Bull$hit is a Financial Superpower

If you're even remotely interested in personal finance, Google's algorithm has almost certainly served up countless ads for scammy investing courses on YouTube.

You know the ones I am talking about. The ads where a 30-something dude is holding his iPhone in selfie mode, walking through a luxury mansion and promising that if you give him 60 seconds of your time, he'll teach you how to get rich trading stocks.

YouTube doesn't let you skip the ad for 7-seconds, but honestly, it only takes me 1 second for my bullshit detector to light up like a Christmas tree.

But more than a few people must be falling for these scams. If they weren't, why would the scammers continue pouring money into these ads?

Clearly, a lot of people need to fine-tune their bullshit detector.

Financial Bullshit is everywhere

A 2022 study written by Kienzler et al. titled "Individual differences in susceptibility to financial bullshit" examined how someone's ability to detect financial bullshit impacts their financial well-being.[4]

4 Kienzler, M., Västfjäll, D., & Tinghög, G. (2022). Individual differences in susceptibility to financial bullshit. *Journal of Behavioral and Experimental Finance*, 100655. https://doi.org/10.1016/j.jbef.2022.100655

The researchers define financial bullshit as "*seemingly impressive verbal, financial assertions that are presented as true and meaningful but are actually meaningless*".

People make big claims about how to make easy money without a shred of credible evidence to back up those claims. It's a tale as old as money, but the internet has increased the ease with which a charlatan can reach millions of people with their bullshit financial claims. If you spend any amount of time on the internet, you are guaranteed to be exposed to financial bullshit.

However, it's important to understand that financial bullshit is not exclusively an online phenomenon. Plenty of bullshitters in the financial services industry will make big claims and use confusing jargon to convince you to invest in their expensive, underperforming mutual fund or buy their questionable financial product.

To quote Kienzler et al.

> *"Pseudo-profound bullshit, in the form of empty talk, lingo and jargon, is commonly experienced by consumers when seeking out financial products and services."*

Measuring financial bullshit

Kienzler et al. surveyed 1,058 people to measure each respondent's:

1. Likeliness to believe financial bullshit
2. Financial well-being
3. Money management habits
4. Financial knowledge

To measure someone's likeliness to believe financial bullshit, respondents were given a list of actually profound quotes about money & finances from historical figures like Milton Friedman and Benjamin Franklin and randomly generated bullshit statements. Respondents measured each quote on a scale of 1-6, with 1 being the lowest score and not at all meaningful and 6 being the highest score and incredibly meaningful.

Here's an example from the study of an actually profound statement from a financial expert.

> "*Finance is not merely about making money. It's about achieving our deep goals and protecting the fruits of our labor.*" – Robert Shiller

Here's an example of a random bullshit statement.

> "*Freedom and space transform the abstract meaning of money.*"

To measure financial well-being, respondents were asked if they agree with a number of statements that speak to financial anxiety and security, such as "*After making a decision, I am anxious whether I was right or wrong*".

To measure money-management habits, respondents were asked various questions about the state of their finances, like whether they had a maxed-out credit card and how often they pay bills on time.

Finally, to measure financial knowledge, respondents were asked whether various statements were true or false. Examples included "*When you buy a bond, you are lending a company money*" or "*Diversification means combining different investment types into a portfolio to reduce risks and increase returns*".

Who is most likely to fall for financial bullshit?

Kienzler et al. found that 86% of respondents scored above zero on the financial bullshit scale—meaning they could, to some degree, spot financial bullshit when they see it.

Who was more likely to fall for financial bullshit?

- Younger people
- Men
- People with a high income
- Those who scored lower on cognitive reflection and financial knowledge
- Overconfident people

So, if you are a 20-something male making a six-figure income with a massive ego, be careful because you are a prime target for financial bullshit artists.

The link between falling for bullshit and financial well-being

One of the important findings from the paper was that falling for financial bullshit did not mean someone was any more likely to feel anxious about their finances—ignorance is bliss.

Those who were more likely to believe financial bullshit were less able to assess the claims made about various financial products or services. This makes them vulnerable to the bullshit artists within the financial services industry.

This book serves as a guide to avoiding investment bullshit.

- In part 1 of the book, I will present the evidence in support of a rational investment portfolio of index funds that is diversified between stocks and bonds and different geographic locations.
- In part 2, I will examine the various bullshit arguments that people will make in an attempt to get you to invest in assets other than index funds. I cover topics ranging from stocking picking to Cryptocurrencies and everything in between.
- In part 3, I review common and recurring investment narratives that bullshitters will use to tempt you to try and time the market. I present the evidence that shows why the rational investor sticks to their plan no matter how scary the narrative of the day happens to be.

Investing is not as complicated as most people think. The real difficulty is tuning out the bullshit over the 40-60 years you are likely to have money invested.

Chapter 2:
Why Invest Your Money?

Before we discuss "how" to invest your money, we should spend some time answering a more important question "Why invest your money at all?"

Here's how an economist would answer that question. Investing allows us to defer consumption today and convert it into future consumption—to which, you might be saying, "Huh?" Remember, economists, are terrible communicators. That's why I am here to translate.

Here's a rational explanation to why we invest. If you invest $100 today, that means you are not spending that $100 on food, entertainment, or travel (consumption). After 30 years, that $100 grows into $1,984 and can be used to buy (consume) whatever you want.

Hidden in this explanation are four essential investment lessons.

Lesson 1: Understanding opportunity cost

The first lesson is what economists call "opportunity cost". Here is a formal definition of opportunity cost according to Investopedia: "Opportunity costs represent the potential benefits an individual, investor, or business misses out on when choosing one alternative over another."[5]

The first thing you need to know about opportunity cost is that it can't be avoided, only minimized. Every choice will have an opportunity cost. Your job is to minimize the opportunity cost of your choices.

---

5 Fernando, J. (2019, June 25). Understanding Opportunity Cost. Investopedia. https://www.investopedia.com/terms/o/opportunitycost.asp

Let's go back to that decision of whether to use your $100 to buy something today or invest it so you can buy things in the future. Either decision has an opportunity cost. If you choose to spend the $100, you are choosing to give up $1,984 worth of consumption 30 years from now. If you choose to invest the $100, then your opportunity cost is $100 in current consumption.

Lesson 2: The longer your keep money invested, the wealthier you become

This brings us to our second investment lesson: a dollar today is worth more than a dollar tomorrow. Economists refer to this concept as "the time value of money". Here's a simple way to think of the time value of money...suppose I offer you two options:

Option 1: I give you $10,000 right now.

Option 2: I give you $10,000 in one year.

Any rational person would choose option 1 because $10,000 today is worth more than $10,000 a year from now. The reason you would take the $10,000 today is that you could invest $10,000 today and grow it to more than $10,000 a year from now. If I give you $10,000 today, and then you invest that money in a low-cost index fund, and your investment grows by 19% a year from now, you would have $11,000.

The time value of money highlights one of the golden rules of investing: to maximize wealth, keep your money invested for as long as possible. You may have heard the phrase "time in the market beats timing the market." In part three of this book, I will explain in detail why this is the case. But for now, hold onto this message; The only three things you can control as an investor are the following:

1. How much money you invest
2. What you choose to invest your money in
3. How long you keep your money invested

Everything else is beyond your control and not worth the mental energy thinking about.

Lesson 3: Let compound interest do the heavy lifting for you

Since you bought a book about investing, I am going to assume you have heard the term "compound interest" before.

Here's a formal definition of compound interest, again courtesy of Investopedia: "Compound interest is the interest earned on your original investment plus all the interest earned on the interest that has accumulated over time."[6]

Put simply: compound interest is when your interest starts earning interest.

- If you invest $100 today and earn a 10% return on investment per year, then after one year, you would have $110.
- $100 would be your original investment, and $10 would be your return on that original investment.
- After two years, you would have $121.

6 Kagan, J. (2019). Compound interest definition. Investopedia. https://www.investopedia.com/terms/c/compoundinterest.asp

To understand compound interest, let's break down how we arrived at $121 after year two.

- $100 would be your original investment
- $10 would be from the return on that original investment in year 1 ($100 X 10%)
- The next $10 would be from the return on that original investment in year 2 ($100 X 10%)
- The final $1 would be the return on your investment gains from year 1 ($10 X 10%)

Each year you keep your money invested, your money grows faster because this year's gains are building on the gains from previous years. More years invested = more compound interest.

At the beginning of this chapter, I showed an example where a $100 investment today could be worth $1,984 in 30 years. I arrived at this calculation using compound interest. I could bore you with the formula for calculating compound interest, but I won't. You don't need to become an economist, you simply need to understand the basic concepts and let computers do the calculations for you. You can find a number of free compound interest calculators on Google that make the job of estimating compounded investment returns foolproof.

Most compound interest calculators will ask you to enter the following information.

1. Your initial investment
2. How often you'll make new investments going forward (weekly, monthly, annually)
3. How much you'll invest at each time interval
4. How many years you'll keep your money invested
5. Your assumed rate of return

If you start with a $100 investment, never invest another dollar, and earn a 10% return on investment per year, after 30 years, you have $1,984.

Notice that four out of five of these variables are, to some degree, in your control.

1. You can decide how much you want to invest to start.
2. You can decide how often you'll make new investments
3. You can decide how much you'll invest when you do make new investments.
4. You can control how long you keep your money invested.

The only variable you can't control is what your annual return on investment will be. This leads us into our fourth essential investing lesson.

Lesson 4: How to make realistic assumptions about investment returns

A lot of new investors overestimate their future return on investment. This is a problem because it tricks you into thinking you need to invest less than you really need to in order to hit your savings goals.

Let's say you're starting from scratch and want to have a $1 million portfolio 30 years from now. The question is, how much money do you need to invest every month to achieve that goal?

To answer that, you need to make an assumption about what your future investment returns will be. To be clear, this is an unknowable number, so all we can hope to do is make the most educated guess possible.

Most investors use past returns to estimate their future return on investments. So, if you were investing in an S&P 500 index fund, you might assume you'll earn 10.5% per year because at the time I write this, the historical average annual return of the S&P 500 index is 10.5%.

A 10.5% rate of return would mean you would need to save $394 per month for the next 30 years to build a $1 million portfolio. But what if your investment returns were only 8% per year? Well, in that scenario, you would only have $587,201. Earning 2.5% less per year means you are more than 40% short of your goal.

You need to take care and make conservative estimates about your return on investment if you hope to hit your goals.

Making rational assumptions about future expected returns is a complicated and imprecise business. Forecasters use data points like what type of assets you're investing in, the current price of those assets, where you live to make a forecast of long-term expected returns.

Forecasts are a fancy way of saying "guess".

Remember, future investment returns are unknowable, so these forecasts of future returns are nothing but educated guesses. That is why I like to take the average forecast made by the investment firms that I trust when making assumptions about my future return on investment.

As a simple example, let's say you were investing in the U.S. stock market and you wanted to find an estimate for the future returns of U.S. stocks. You might take the average forecasted returns of the three largest asset managers in the U.S: Vanguard, Blackrock, and Fidelity.

In this hypothetical example, let's say each firm's expected future annual return on U.S. stocks was as follows.

- Vanguard: 3%
- Blackrock: 4%
- Fidelity: 5%

The average of these three forecasts is 4%. In this scenario, 4% might be our best guess for the future return on our investments. This, of course, will be wrong, but it's an average of the best information we have available to us today. It might be tempting to use historical average returns as our expected future returns but to quote a cliche in the investment industry, "past performance is not indicative of future results."

Chapter 3: Why Invest in Stocks?

Financial services is a $22.5 trillion industry worldwide.[7] Like any business, companies managing your money make their money by selling you products. Some of them are fantastic products that are essential to building and keeping wealth. Others are expensive, confusing, and unnecessary. I'll leave it to you to guess which type of product make these financial firms the most money.

The thesis of this book is simple: buy a handful of low-cost index funds and hold onto them until you reach retirement age.

Not all index funds invest in stocks. If there is a market for a particular asset—like bonds, there is an index fund to track that market. As a point of clarification, when I am referring to a bond index fund, I will explicitly say "bond index fund". If I say "index fund", assume I'm referring to equity index funds that track a stock market. The reason for this is quite simple: stocks are the most rational investment choice to build long-term passive wealth.

In this chapter, we will explore two questions in further detail.

1. Why invest in stocks?
2. How much of your portfolio should you invest in stocks?

---

7 *What Percentage of the Global Economy Is the Financial Services Sector?* (2021, September 30). Investopedia. https://www.investopedia.com/ask/answers/030515/what-percentage-global-economy-comprised-financial-services-sector.asp

Why invest in stocks in the first place?

Let's start with a clear understanding of what you're doing when you invest in stocks. When you buy a stock, you become a part-owner in a business. If the business makes a profit, you share in those profits as a partial owner of the business. As long as we live in a capitalist economic system, owning profitable businesses is the simplest path to accumulating wealth.

You may have already noticed me using the phrase "long-term" a lot. I'm going to continue using this phrase throughout the book because stocks are a terrible short-term investment but an incredible long-term investment to build wealth.

Stocks make for a lousy short-term investment because they are incredibly volatile (large swings up and down.) There have been single years (1931) where the S&P 500 lost more than 43% of its value and single days (1987) where the S&P 500 lost more than 22% of its value.

Any investment with that level of volatility makes for a dangerous short-term investment. Say you invested $10,000 in the stock market and needed to use that money a year from now to pay for your kid's college tuition. There is a very real possibility that your $10,000 investment could drop to $5,000 or lower a year from now. What a devastating mistake that impacts both you and your child.

If you are a long-term investor—think decades, not years—then that level of volatility from year to year becomes inconsequential. Long-term investors are not concerned about what happens over the next year. They are focused on what is likely to occur over the next 20 years. On that front, I have excellent news. At the time I write this sentence, nobody has ever lost money from buying an S&P 500 index fund and sitting on it for 20 years. The longer you hold, the better your investment returns are likely to be.

So, why do we invest in stocks? Because in a capitalist society, the most tried and true path to building wealth is to own profitable businesses, which is what we do when we invest in stocks. That being said, stocks can be highly volatile. We should only invest money in the stock market if we are prepared to keep that money invested for a decade or more.

Why it's even more important for young people to invest in stocks

Common investing advice is that the number of years you have until retirement is the most important factor when deciding how much of your portfolio should be allocated to risky assets (like stocks) and safer assets (like bonds).

If you were to ask a financial advisor why young people should invest more in stocks than older people, they would point to the data we just reviewed and tell you that investors who buy an S&P 500 index fund and sit on it for 20-30 years don't lose money. In the finance field, the benefits of this long-term holding period are referred to as "time diversification". The central idea is that longer holding periods make investing in stocks less risky.

If you were to ask an economist why young people should invest more in stocks than those in or nearing retirement, they would tell you it's all about building a balanced portfolio. Young people and older people likely have a similar amount of wealth, just in radically different forms.

- The old are rich in financial capital. After a lifetime of saving and investing, people in their 60s and 70s tend to be flush with cash, stocks, bonds, and real estate.
- The young are rich in human capital. Your human capital is your ability to earn a paycheck. The more paychecks you have left to collect in your life, the more human capital you own.

If you're 25 and plan on working until 65, you have as many as 1,040 paychecks left to collect in your life. These paychecks you have yet to collect are nothing but a stream of future cash flows. Like any stream of future cash flows, economists can put a present value on them. If you have 40 years of future cash flows (paychecks) to collect, the present value is probably as big as a retiree's 401k + the value of their house.

If you have a 9-5 job, the paychecks you collect look a lot like coupon payments from a bond. Every two weeks, the same amount of money hits your bank account like clockwork, just like a bond.

Economists look at your total portfolio of assets as your financial capital (stocks, cash bonds, etc.) + your human capital (value of future paychecks).

Young people should load up on stocks because they are potentially sitting on millions of dollars' worth of "bond-like" human capital. In comparison, they probably have very little risky financial capital like stocks. The economist would look at this and say that the young person's total portfolio (financial + human capital) is too concentrated in bonds (future paychecks).

An economist would say that young people must over-invest in stocks because they already have too many bonds in their portfolio of human capital. That means their financial capital needs more stocks to balance out their total portfolio.

If your human capital is the present value of future paychecks, what happens when you retire? You have no more paychecks, and your human capital is $0 (assuming you don't work in retirement). As you age and your human capital dries up, you begin de-risking your financial capital.

By the time your human capital is worth $0, you transition to living off your financial capital. To maintain a properly diversified portfolio, you should have a more balanced mix of risky stocks and less risky bonds.

Why not stay heavily invested in stocks during retirement?

Because the stock market remains incredibly risky. If 100% of your retirement income comes from the stock market, what happens if your portfolio gets cut in half two years into retirement?

You'll run out of money.

Your total portfolio should always have a balance of stocks and bonds. Stock to grow and bonds to provide steady, predictable income. When you're young, your bonds come in the form of human capital. As you age and you have fewer paychecks to collect, your bonds should come in the form of literal bonds in your portfolio of financial capital.

Chapter 4:
Index Funds are the Rational way to Invest in Stocks

This book is not exactly a "beginner's" guide to investing, so I'm going to assume that you are at least somewhat familiar with what an index fund is. But we must have a shared understanding of what an index fund is and why it's the perfect tool to build passive wealth before we go any further on this journey together.

Let's start with some basic terminology. Specifically, two terms are often used interchangeably but are distinctly different. I am talking about index funds and ETFs.

ETFs or Exchange Traded Funds are investment funds that can be bought and sold on stock exchanges in the same way as individual stocks. Index funds replicate an index of assets like stocks or bonds. For example, an S&P 500 index fund replicates the S&P 500 index, a list of the 505 largest companies in the U.S. as measured by their market capitalization.

Index funds are defined by their passive investment strategy of replicating a particular index of assets. ETFs are defined as a specific structure of an investment fund.

Not all Index funds are ETFs, and not all ETFs are index funds.

Many index funds are not ETFs but are structured as traditional mutual funds. This means they are not bought on stock exchanges but directly through investment fund companies.

Many ETFs do not follow an indexing strategy. This means they have active fund managers picking and choosing assets rather than following a passive investment strategy.

In this book, when I refer to "index funds", I am referring to ETF index funds. ETF index funds are much more accessible compared to index mutual funds, especially for DIY investors.

It's also important to remember that index funds don't only refer to stocks. There are indices that track just about every asset you can think of, such as stocks, bonds, commodities, and Real Estate Investment Trusts (REITs), to name a few. If there is an index that tracks an asset class, you can be sure there's an index fund replicating it.

Not all index funds are created equal.

Just because an ETF calls itself an "index fund" does not mean it is a good investment.

There are more indexes and index ETFs than I could ever keep track of. I like to separate index funds into three categories.

1. Broad-based index funds.
2. Niche index funds.
3. Fake index funds.

Broad-based index funds invest in all of a particular asset class in a specific geographic region. An S&P 500 index fund invests in the majority of the U.S. stock market.

Niche index funds invest in "*alternative*" assets and subsections of a broad-based index. For example, you could invest in an index fund that tracks an index of technology companies.

Niche index funds, by their nature, are much more concentrated than broad-based index funds and therefore have a higher variance in possible outcomes. They could do great, or they could do terribly.

Fake index funds are when investment firms create an index out of thin air. Then they create a product that tracks this newly-created index and ta-da! You have an "index fund". I dedicate an entire chapter in part two of this book to fake index funds to help you understand why they are dangerous and how to spot them in the wild.

Index funds eliminate unnecessary risk

There are two types of risk investors have to be aware of:

1. Systematic risk.
2. Idiosyncratic risk.

Systematic risk is the risk that the entire economy and stock market will experience a downturn. Systematic risk is something anyone investing in the stock market accepts. They accept this risk because the expected (not guaranteed) outcome of investing in stocks is positive. This is where the term "*no risk, no reward*" comes from.

Idiosyncratic risk is the risk that an individual company (for those who pick stocks) or a specific sector (for those who choose niche index funds) faces. If you invested in a technology index fund, you would be exposed to the broader stock market risk and risks that are specific to the technology industry.

Idiosyncratic risks can be managed through proper diversification. By proper diversification, I mean investing in broad-based index funds that are diversified by asset class and geography (more on that later).

If your goal is to maximize risk-adjusted expected returns, broad-based index funds make much more sense than buying niche index funds.

The efficient market theory

The most important academic research supporting index funds as a rational investment is the "efficient market theory". If the stock market is efficient, then all available information is already reflected in current stock prices.

- If the stock market is efficient, it's impossible to pick stocks and "*beat the market*" in the long run, therefore the only sensible way to invest is to buy the whole market through index funds.
- If the market is inefficient, active managers can outperform the stock market by picking the "*good stocks*" and staying away from the "*bad stocks.*"

We can thank Nobel prize-winning economist Eugene Fama for introducing the concept of efficient markets in his 1970 paper "Efficient Capital Markets: a Review of Theory and Empirical Work.[8]"

Is the stock market perfectly efficient all the time?

Of course not. There is irrationality baked into the stock market. You need only look at the rise of "meme-stocks" in 2020 to understand how irrational investors can be.

If markets were completely inefficient, then the most skilled stock pickers and Wall Street managers would be able to exploit those inefficiencies and consistently outperform the market.

---

8 Fama, E. F. (1970). Efficient Capital Markets: a Review of Theory and Empirical Work. The Journal of Finance, 25(2), 383–417. https://doi.org/10.2307/2325486

Standard & Poor's keeps a "Scorecard[9]" that measures how actively-managed investment funds perform compared to the local stock market index. At the time I write this, over the past 10 years:

- 83% of U.S. funds underperformed the S&P 500
- 83% of Canadian funds underperformed the TSX
- 85% of European funds underperformed the S&P Europe 350

In part two of this book, we will dive much deeper into these numbers when we review the odds of successfully picking stocks or fund managers.

So, what does this tell us?

Even though markets are not perfectly efficient, we should invest as if they are. Investors who pick and choose stocks, time the market and carry on as if the market were inefficient, consistently underperform the market.

The beautiful design of index funds makes them perfect for building passive wealth

What makes index funds incredible is not their historically exceptional returns or the broad diversification, or even their low costs, it's their passive nature. Index funds adopt a passive strategy of tracking the market. Index funds work best when the investors who buy them also embrace a passive strategy of buying and holding.

If you bought an S&P 500 index fund 10 years ago and never checked your balance, you would have outperformed 82.5% of active investment fund managers. These are smart, successful, powerful people with an army

9 *SPIVA | S&P Dow Jones Indices*. (n.d.). Www.spglobal.com. Retrieved March 28, 2022, from https://www.spglobal.com/spdji/en/research-insights/spiva/

of analysts at their disposal. And you would have had better investment returns than them if you just bought an index fund and went about your life not thinking about it.

Above all else, the power of index investing is that it frees you from thinking about your investments. No checking your portfolio every day. No watching CNBC or following "finance Twitter". No worrying about what's happening with inflation or interest rates or any of the distractions that so many investors get sucked into.

Freeing yourself from these burdens allows you to focus on the most important aspect of building wealth: finding more money to invest.

The secret to building wealth is not in picking investments that outperform, but in widening the gap between your income and expenses and then investing the difference. The wider the gap, the more you can invest. The more you can invest, the more wealth you will build.

Most investors fail to build wealth because they do the reverse. They try (and fail) to outperform the market, which is a time-consuming activity. This leaves them with less time and energy to focus on building side hustles or starting businesses that could increase their income and allow them to invest more money.

The lesson?

Don't turn your investments into a part-time job. The most likely outcome is that you will lose the two most important assets in life: time and money. Embrace the fact that you won't outperform the market. This is not a sign of weakness or a waiving of a white flag but a sign of wisdom. Buy a handful of low-cost index funds and start dedicating your talents and mental calories to the most crucial aspect of the wealth-building process: saving and investing as high of a percentage of your income as you can.

Chapter 5: The 20-year Rule to Investing

My wife and I set up an investment account to help save for the cost of our son's education. I invest the money on his behalf because he is two years old, and toddlers have no business investing in the stock market.

Unfortunately, a lot of investors act like toddlers.

They can't sit still, only focus on what is directly in front of them, and change their minds every five seconds. My toddler will scream bloody murder for an apple, only to take one bite, throw it away and start crying for cookies. (*Yes, I have eaten my fair share of half-eaten apples off the floor.*)

Toddler investors jump into the stock market, thinking it's an easy way to make quick money, only to jump ship when the water gets choppy.

If you want to be a great investor, you need to learn to sit still and do nothing. You need to learn to invest like an adult.

A stock market secret the financial media won't tell you

The financial media act as a sort of cheerleader for the stock market. Which is a very useful and necessary service. Most people find the stock market intimidating, scary, or even corrupt. When the average person thinks about the stock market, images of the financial crisis or some shady white dudes in tacky suits float through their mind.

This is a shame because the stock market—if used like an adult—is the best way for middle-class workers to build wealth.

Here's the secret the financial media won't tell you about the stock market.

The stock market is one of the worst places to put your money unless you keep it there for decades.

Stocks are a terrible short-term investment but an incredible long-term investment.

Stocks make for a lousy short-term investment because they are incredibly volatile (large swings up and down). It's possible for the stock market to lose half its value in a single year. Lousy isn't even the right word. Dangerous is a better word for it.

If I invest $10,000 in the stock market to pay for the future cost of my child's education, there is a very real possibility that the investment could be worth $5,000 a year from now. If that happens, I'm not worried because my son is only two. If that happened, when he was 17, that could have devastating implications for his financial future.

If you need your money days, weeks, months, or even a few years from now, the stock market is a dangerous place to keep your money. Don't get greedy with the money you'll need to spend in the near future.

Grown-up investors think in decades, not years

Here is my favorite Warren Buffett quote:

> *"The first rule of an investment is don't lose money. And the second rule of an investment is don't forget the first rule. And that's all the rules there are."*

Grown-up investors take Buffett's golden rule of investing to heart. If you follow the data, there is a tried and true investing philosophy that ensures you follow Buffett's rules to investing: ***Buy index funds and hold onto them for 20+ years.***

No investor in history has ever lost money when they buy an S&P 500 index fund and sit on it for 20 years. That's not hyperbole—it's a fact[10].

The S&P 500 had negative returns in 31% of years from 1872-2019. Nearly one in three years, the stock market provides negative returns. But that should only scare toddler investors.

Zoom out, and everything comes into focus.

Grown-up investors who hold the S&P 500 for 20 years and reinvest the dividends have never lost money between 1872-2019—and yes, that includes inflation.

Here's a chart that shows the total real returns of the S&P 500 for each decade from 1880 to the 2010s.

Decade Beginning In	S&P 500 Total Real Returns
1880	8.3%
1890	5.5%
1900	7.7%
1910	-1.9%
1920	16.2%
1930	2.2%
1940	3.4%
1950	16.7%
1960	5.1%
1970	-1.5%
1980	11.7%
1990	14.8%
2000	-3.4%
2010	10.8%

10 *U.S. Stock Market Returns - 1870s to Present.* (2018, March 25). The Measure of a Plan. https://themeasureofaplan.com/us-stock-market-returns-1870s-to-present/

As you will notice, there are only three decades (1910,1970 & 2000) in which the S&P 500 had real negative returns.

This tells us two things.

1. Buying and holding index funds is as good a strategy to outpace inflation as you will find (more on that later in the book).
2. Investors who buy and hold for 20 years or longer get rewarded.

But most investors, even index investors, fail to sit still that long.

- They get nervous about market crashes, so they sell—right before the market unexpectedly takes off and has some of its biggest gains.
- They get bored and sell their index funds in exchange for the hot new investment idea trending on social media—just before the trending investment is about to blow up.
- They get greedy and use dangerous tools like leverage to magnify their gains—but it ends up blowing up in their face.

So, if you want to be a great investor, invest like an adult: think in terms of decades, not years.

Chapter 6: Diversification Means Buying Different Assets in Different Places

If you want to be a great investor, embrace these four words: Buy, diversify, never sell.

Those four words are the mission statement of this entire book. To this point, we have spent a lot of time discussing why you need to "buy". Now, let's talk about diversification.

"Diversify your portfolio." It's a phrase that has become so common that even people who have never invested a single dollar in their life have heard it.

Diversification is a way of managing risk. "Diversifying your portfolio" is another way of saying "don't put all your eggs in one basket." If you have a dozen eggs and decide to carry them all in one basket, you risk losing all of your eggs if you drop the basket. If you have a dozen eggs and put each one in its own basket, even if you drop a basket and break an egg, you still have 11 more eggs.

The same concept applies to investing. If you take your life savings and invest it in a single company, what happens if that company goes bankrupt? You lose your life savings.

If you take your life savings and invest it in hundreds or even thousands of companies, what happens if one of those companies goes bankrupt? Probably nothing. The more you diversify, the less impact a single asset will have on your portfolio.

Diversifying your portfolio is a smart and simple way to manage investment risk.

But, how do you actually go about diversifying an investment portfolio?

Let's discuss diversification using language that does not require a Ph.D. in economics to understand.

The three essential elements of a diversified portfolio

For index investors, diversification means taking the following three actions.

1. Investing in different types of assets.
2. Investing in assets in different countries.
3. Buying all of the assets in each asset class you invest in.

#1: Investing in different types of assets

If you invest in stocks, bonds, and real estate, that is a form of diversification because you own three unique assets with different risk levels and expected returns. These assets are not perfectly correlated. That means if the stock market is down 5%, bonds probably aren't down 5%, and in fact, they may have even increased in value.

Owning different types of assets lowers the volatility (big swings up and down) in your portfolio.

In the 2008-2009 financial crisis, stocks lost more than 40% of their value. At the same time, high-quality bonds not only held their value but increased. Having a chunk of your portfolio that increases in value during turbulent times can prevent you from making a fear-based decision of selling your stocks and turning a paper loss into a real loss.

#2: Investing in assets in different countries

This is the part of diversification that most investors forget about.

Let's return to the metaphor of not putting all your eggs in one basket when it comes to diversifying your portfolio which has two meanings.

1. Don't put all your money into one asset class.
2. Don't put all your money in one country.

We just talked about buying different types of assets. Now let's talk about why you want to buy assets in different countries.

If you live in the U.S, chances are that most of your money is invested in U.S. stocks and U.S. bonds, which makes sense. People invest in what they know because it makes them feel safe.

If you invest all of your money in a single country and that country's economy suffers, you will have poor investment returns. If your money is spread throughout multiple countries, even if one country is underperforming, that might be offset by another country outperforming.

Beyond gaining exposure to other economies, a globally diversified portfolio can ensure you don't miss out on the companies that will drive the stock market in the future.

A 2019 paper written by Vanguard found that investors who allocate roughly half of their portfolio to international stocks experience less volatility.[11] This finding fits with the theory of diversification. A well-diversified

11 Donaldson, S., Ahluwalia, H., Renzi-Ricci, G., Zhu, V., & Aleksandrovich, A. (n.d.). *Global equity investing: The benefits of diversification and sizing your allocation.* Retrieved March 28, 2022, from https://corporate.vanguard.com/content/dam/corp/research/pdf/Global-equity-investing-The-benefits-of-diversification-and-sizing-your-allocation-US-ISGGEB_042021_Online.pdf

portfolio (which includes global diversification) will be less volatile than a highly concentrated portfolio.

When you buy assets in different countries, it lowers the level of concentration in your portfolio.

The U.S. stock market makes up roughly 56% of the global stock market. That means if you invest only in U.S. stocks, you're ignoring 44% of all publically traded companies you could be investing in.

Let's look at two Vanguard index funds (not an endorsement to buy either fund) to compare the number of companies they invest in.

- VOO[12], an index fund that tracks the S&P 500, holds 507 U.S. stocks.
- VT[13], an index fund that tracks the global stock market holds 9,364 stocks.

With VOO, the 10 largest stocks make up more than 30% of the portfolio. With VT, the 10 largest stocks make up 15% of the portfolio. Fun fact, 9/10 of the top 10 stocks in each fund are the same (mega-cap U.S. stocks like Microsoft).

Look beyond your own backyard when diversifying your investments. It's a big world out there.

---

12 *Vanguard ETF Profile | Vanguard.* (n.d.). Investor.vanguard.com. https://investor.vanguard.com/etf/profile/VOO

13 *Vanguard ETF Profile | Vanguard.* (n.d.). Investor.vanguard.com. Retrieved March 28, 2022, from https://investor.vanguard.com/etf/profile/VT

#3: Buying all of the assets in each asset class, you invest in

Finally, on the point of buying all the assets in the asset class you invest in can be done simply by buying index funds. We just reviewed two solid examples of index funds. Buying 5–7 U.S. stocks does not look much like diversification when you compare it to the over 500 stocks in the S&P 500 and the 9,000+ you can invest in through a global index fund.

As you can see, the three elements of diversification can be easily achieved with a handful of domestic and international index funds.

Yes, you will have to do some research upfront to figure out which funds and what weighting of those funds is appropriate for you. Over the next few chapters, we will cover many of the important factors you need to weigh when constructing your portfolio.

Chapter 7: How Much of a Portfolio Should be Allocated to Risky vs. Safe Assets?

The perfect investment portfolio is the one with the highest returns that you can stay invested in.

You must understand the two components of that sentence. First, maximize investment returns and second, minimize the odds that you'll sell your investments—either by necessity or by choice—prematurely.

Investment returns and risk are tied at the hip; higher returns, by definition, require you to take on more risk. The kneejerk reaction would be to conclude that you should load up on risky assets like stocks.

However, the more risk in a portfolio, the more likely you are to sell your investments prematurely. This is a problem because the only foolproof way to become a great investor is to buy and hold for decades. Adding less risky assets, like bonds, into a portfolio reduces the expected returns but lowers volatility.

It's important to understand that people sell their portfolios prematurely for two reasons.

1. **Their portfolio exceeds their *capacity* to take on risk** (they are forced to sell).
2. **Their portfolio exceeds their *willingness* to take on risk** (they choose to sell).

Let's break down what that means and how you can maximize your investment returns and stay invested for the long term.

Factors that impact your capacity to take on investment risk

The golden rule of building wealth is that your income must always be greater than your expenses.

If your income falls below the cost to fund your lifestyle—like if you lose your job— you open up the possibility of being forced to sell your investments prematurely to pay the bills.

That's a situation you never want to be in.

Increasing your capacity to take on investment risk means minimizing the odds that you will ever find yourself in a situation where your expenses are greater than your income.

Two factors primarily drive your capacity to take on risk.

1. Your human capital.
2. Your financial plan.

Starting with your human capital, aka your ability to earn income, which, as we covered in Chapter 3, is an asset.

Once again, ask yourself how risky is my income?

All else being equal, the more secure your job is, the more risk capacity you have in your portfolio because your odds of losing your income are low. On the other hand, if you have very little job security, you have less capacity to take on investment risk.

Diversification of income is also important.

If you live in a two-income household and each person's income could independently cover the household living expenses, then you have a higher capacity to take on risk. Another way to diversify your income is to build a second income stream by starting a side hustle or side business that provides income independent of your primary income.

Basic financial planning also plays a role in increasing your capacity to take on investment risk.

Reducing your living expenses, paying down debt, and ensuring you have enough cash on hand to weather a job loss.

Here's a simple approach to estimating how much cash you might need to keep on hand in case of an emergency.

1. Track your average monthly living expenses.
2. Research your industry and come up with a conservative estimate of how many months it would take to land a good job in your field.
3. Multiply your average monthly expenses by the number of months to find a new job.

If you spend $5,000 per month and a conservative estimate for how long it would take to find a new job is 6 months, then you need at least $30,000 in cash to cover your living expenses in between jobs without selling your investments prematurely.

Yes, that $30,000 would be earning more if it was invested, but that is the wrong way to think about an emergency fund. We should rename financial emergency funds and call them what they are: an insurance policy against losing your job. The opportunity cost of the cash sitting in your emergency fund is the insurance premium you pay to ensure that cash is there when you need it.

The more months' worth of living expenses you have in cash, the more capacity you have to invest in risky assets like stocks with the rest of your money.

Assessing your willingness to take on risk

Your willingness to take on risk comes down to psychology.

Some people are naturally comfortable taking on investment risk, while others would rather stick their money under a mattress than deal with the volatility on the stock market.

You must balance your willingness to take on risk with the actual risk in your investment portfolio. If your portfolio has more risk than you can handle, you are likely to get spooked and sell when the market crashes.

Your first step is to do some research to understand where your risk tolerance currently stands. Vanguard's online risk assessment tool is a great place to start.[14]

Here are a few ways you might be able to increase your willingness to take on risk.

Think about what problems in your life investing can solve

When I met my wife, she had all her money in a checking account, earning 0%. She had zero comfort with investment risk and distrusted anyone in the financial services industry who tried to convince her to invest her money.

---

14 *Vanguard - Investor Questionnaire - Terms and conditions of use.* (n.d.). Retirementplans.vanguard.com. https://retirementplans.vanguard.com/VGApp/pe/PubQuizActivity?Step=start

Fast forward to today, and my wife has a six-figure, self-managed investment account and is putting more money into the market every month.

What changed?

One day we reviewed our workplace pension plans, and we realized that her pension would allow her to retire at 55 while mine would allow me to retire at 65. Neither of us liked the idea of having a 10-year gap in our retirement timelines, it was important for us to be able to retire at the same time.

This was a problem that investing could fix.

Once we ran through the numbers, and it became clear that the easiest way to ensure we retire at the same time was by investing early, often, and aggressively, she instantly warmed up to the idea of taking on investment risk.

The same thing happened when our son was born.

We looked at the numbers and realized how much more our son's college fund would be by the time he turns 18 if we invest aggressively while he is young.

Notice, that the motivation for my wife to embrace investment risk was not to "get rich" but to increase the well-being of our family. This mental shift completely changed her willingness to invest and hang in there during periods of high volatility.

Use an investment advisor

These days it's very fashionable to bash the idea of using an investment advisor. While the financial services industry has earned its poor reputation, a quality investment advisor more than pays for their fees.

Russell Investments, a Canadian investment firm published a study showing investors who used an advisor had a 2.88% higher annual return on investment than DIY investors.[15] To be clear, this outperformance is not due to the advisor picking some market-beating investment.

Investors using an advisor outperformed because the advisor saves the investor from themselves during periods of high volatility. When the market crashes, many people will make a snap decision, driven by fear, to sell their portfolios.

But what if you had an investment advisor you could call before you hit the sell button? Unless the advisor completely misjudged your risk tolerance, they should be able to talk you off the ledge and save you from blowing up your portfolio.

Compare that to the DIY investor who gets all of their investment advice off Twitter, which rewards hyperbolic reactions like "THIS IS AN ECONOMIC CRISIS WORSE THAN THE GREAT DEPRESSION."

All else being equal, which one of these investors do you think is more likely to stay invested for the long run?

Go on a financial media diet

The investor who consistently puts money into a diversified portfolio of index funds and never sells will be the investor who maximizes their long-term passive wealth.

---

15 *Value of a Financial Advisor | Russell Investments.* (n.d.). Russellinvestments.com. https://russellinvestments.com/us/resources/financial-professionals/value-of-advisor

Unfortunately, the financial services and financial media industries have the exact opposite incentive. They want you to follow every development in the stock market and constantly make trades in your portfolio.

If every user of a commission-free stock trading service bought an S&P 500 index fund and sat on it for 40 years, the brokerage would go broke.

If every financial media company ran the same headline every day that read, "What happened in the stock market today is irrelevant for the long-term investor", the media company would go broke.

What's best for you is to invest your money in a handful of globally diversified index funds and never sell under any circumstance.

That's why the financial media you consume should focus on education rather than hyperbolic headlines.

Chapter 8: How Much of a Portfolio Should be Allocated to Domestic vs International?

Another important question when thinking of diversification is how much of your portfolio should be allocated to domestic vs. international assets?

This is a much more complicated question to answer because tax policies provide strong incentives to overweight domestic stocks.

If tax policy treated domestic and international stocks equally, the rational approach would be to invest the equity portion of your portfolio in a single index fund that tracks the global stock market. An example of an index fund that does this is Vanguard's Total World Stock ETF (not an endorsement of the fund).

A fund like this invests in stock markets around the world based on each country's proportional share of the global stock market. At the time I write this, here are the top 10 countries in Vanguard's Total World Stock ETF and how much of the total portfolio is in each country.

1. U.S. – 59.7%
2. Japan – 6.2%
3. U.K — 4.1%
4. Hong Kong — 3.5%
5. Canada — 2.8%
6. France — 2.6%
7. Switzerland — 2.4%
8. Germany — 2.2%
9. Taiwan — 2%
10. Australia — 1.9%

Looking at these numbers, one thing becomes clear: international diversification is especially important for non-U.S. investors.

Why?

Canadian stocks make up 2.8% of the global stock market. If a Canadian investor allocated 100% of the equity portion of their portfolio to Canadian stocks, they would exclude 97.2% of the global stock market from their portfolio.

U.S. stocks make up 60% of the global stock market. If a U.S. investor allocated 100% of the equity portion of their portfolio to U.S. stocks, they would exclude 40% of the global stock market from their portfolio.

Obviously, U.S. investors need to think about international stocks, but it's even more important for international investors where domestic stocks make up a small portion of the global stock market.

Without tax policy distorting our incentives, the rational way to invest in stocks would be to follow these weightings by country. That means a U.S. investor would allocate 40% of their equities to international stocks, and a Canadian investor would allocate 97.2% of their equities to international stocks.

But we don't live in that kind of world. There are two powerful tax policies that incentivize investors to move away from the perfectly rational global weighted investment strategy.

1. Foreign withholding taxes
2. Preferential taxes for domestic stocks

Beware of withholding taxes

An important consideration when investing in international index funds is withholding taxes, which are taxes levied by a foreign government when an investor receives dividends from a company in that foreign country. If a foreign company pays you a dividend, a portion of that dividend is taxed before it ever gets to you.

The level of withholding tax varies and depends on what agreements (if any) exist between your government and the government of the country where the dividend originated from.

Sadly, you can't avoid withholding taxes completely. If you are going to diversify your portfolio by investing in foreign stocks, withholding taxes are a reality you'll have to deal with.

Before investing in an international ETF, it's important to do your research and find out how much withholding tax you would need to pay on dividends paid to you.

Preferential tax treatments of investing domestically

While withholding taxes act as a disincentive to invest internationally, most governments provide tax incentives to invest in domestic stocks.

I am Canadian, so I will review the issue of tax incentives on domestic dividends from the perspective of a Canadian investor. Many other countries, including the U.S., provide a similar incentive to invest in domestic stocks.

When I invest in a Canadian stock index fund in a taxable account, the dividends paid to me are what are called "eligible dividends". These dividends receive a preferential tax treatment compared to dividends from an ETF that invests in international stocks.

I live in the province of Ontario in Canada, where the highest tax bracket is 53% for provincial and federal taxes combined. If I am in that 53% tax bracket, I would only pay a 39% tax on the "eligible dividends" I receive from publicly traded Canadian companies. Any dividends I receive from international companies would be taxed at 53%.

Here's an example of how powerful these incentives can be at the 53% tax bracket.

- If I received $10,000 in dividends from Canadian companies, I would have roughly $6,100 left after taxes.
- If I received $10,000 in dividends from foreign companies, I would have roughly $4,700 left after taxes.

This provides a powerful incentive for me to allocate more of my portfolio to domestic rather than international stocks.

The rational way to consider international asset allocation

Investing internationally provides greater diversification to a portfolio. But, it comes at the cost of withholding taxes and forgone tax incentives from investing in domestic stocks (when held in a taxable account).

Back to the question, how much of your portfolio should be allocated to domestic and international stocks?

There is no right answer.

If dividends from domestic and international stocks were treated equally, the rational approach for the equity portion of your portfolio would be to invest in one index fund that tracks the global stock market and invests in each country based on that country's share of the global stock market.

- Think of this market-weighted approach as the starting point for your domestic vs. international allocation.

- Then consider the withholding taxes of investing internationally, which provides an incentive to invest more in domestic stocks.
- Then consider any tax incentives of investing domestically, which provides further incentive to invest in domestic stocks.

How much you invest domestically and internationally will depend on what country you live in and how you feel about the incentives I just described.

Chapter 9: Important Factors to Consider When Buying Index Funds

Recall in Chapter 4, I said that I would use the words "index funds" and ETFs interchangeably. Even though not all index funds are sold as ETFs, and not all ETFs follow a passive indexing strategy, the rational investment vehicle most readily available to DIY investors are ETFs that do follow a passive indexing strategy.

In this chapter, I'll review four important factors to look for when choosing which ETFs you want to invest in.

1. Management Expense Ratio (MER)

Index funds have one job: to replicate the performance of a particular index. For example, an S&P 500 index fund is designed to replicate the performance of the S&P 500. That is the job of all S&P 500 index funds.

If all index funds have the same job of tracking a particular index, then the silliest thing you can do is to pay more than you have to for an index fund. That is where Management Expense Ratios (MERs) come into play.

An MER is a fee you pay to the fund, which pays the costs to run the fund. MERs are a percentage of the money you have invested in the fund.

Let's assume the other three factors I'm about to discuss remain equal, and you need to decide between two S&P 500 index funds: one fund that has an MER of 0.20% and another that has an MER of 0.02%.

Which should you choose?

Since these funds do the exact same thing, the only rational choice would be to pick the fund with an MER of 0.02%. Why would you pay one penny more than you have to when deciding between two products that are essentially identical?

Whatever type of index fund you are considering, the first thing to look for is the MER of the various funds that track that index. If you are looking for an index fund that tracks the Canadian stock market, the first place to start is to compare the MER of the various Canadian equity ETFs.

You can't control what happens in the markets, but you can control your investment costs.

2. Commissions

Let's stay on the issue of controlling your investment costs.

Commissions have less to do with the ETF you buy and more to do with the online broker you buy the ETF from. Some online brokerages charge a commission every time you buy an ETF. These fees are often around $5 per transaction.

So, if you spent $100 buying ETFs, you could be charged $5 for that transaction. This can seriously eat into the returns of smaller investors who are investing small amounts of money at a time.

For that reason, before you start your DIY investing journey, you should take your time to find the right online broker that allows you to buy ETFs for the lowest price possible.

3. Fund structure & withholding taxes

I reviewed the issue of withholding taxes in Chapter 8 when we discussed the issue of investing internationally.

All investors who invest in international stocks will need to deal with the issue of withholding taxes.

Non-U.S. investors may have to deal with a second layer of withholding taxes, one applied by the government of the country you invest in and another by the U.S. investor when you invest internationally through a U.S.-listed ETF.

Since I am Canadian, I'll explain the two levels of withholding tax in the Canadian context. If you are not American or Canadian, a similar withholding tax issue will likely be a factor for your investing.

Level 1 (L1) withholding tax: These are withholding taxes levied by a foreign government when a Canadian investor receives dividends from a company in that country.

Level 2 (L2) withholding tax: This is an additional withholding tax (typically 15%) applied by the U.S. government. Level 2 withholding tax applies to dividends paid to a Canadian investor by a Canadian-listed ETF that owns a U.S.-listed ETF. You still have to pay level 1 withholding tax in addition to this 15% withholding tax to the U.S. Government.

Depending on the structure of the ETF, I may have to pay level 1 or level 2 withholding tax when investing in international index funds. That is why it is so important to know if the ETF I am considering investing in holds stocks directly or holds a U.S.-listed ETF. That will be a huge factor in whether level 1 or level 2 withholding taxes apply.

Before investing in an ETF to gain exposure to international stocks, ask your broker or your financial advisor which funds can minimize your withholding taxes.

4. Tracking error

The fourth factor to look for before buying an ETF is the fund's tracking error. Tracking error measures the fund's accuracy in tracking its underlying index. It is the difference between the fund's performance and the performance of the index it seeks to track.

Returning to the example of an S&P 500 index fund, the tracking error tells us how closely the index fund mirrors the performance of the S&P 500. If the S&P 500 returned 10% in a given year and my S&P 500 index fund had a 9% return, the tracking error would be 1%.

Since the entire point of index funds is to track the performance of an index, look for funds that have the lowest tracking error as they are more reliable.

Are these four factors the only things to look for when buying ETFs?

Of course not.

But if you can minimize your investment fees through the MER, commissions, and withholding taxes and find an ETF with a low tracking error, you've likely put yourself in a position to succeed.

Chapter 10:
The #1 Reason People Never Invest Their Money

We began part one of this book by discussing why you should invest in the stock market.

We will conclude this part of the book by discussing why approximately 42% of the adult population has $0 invested in the stock market.[16]

A critical question for this large group of people is, *"why don't they invest?"*

The biggest reason people don't invest

A 2018 paper written by James Choi and Adriana Robertson titled "What Matters to Individual Investors? Evidence from the Horse's Mouth" surveyed 1,013 people to gain a better understanding of the various perceptions the average person has about investing in the stock market.[17]

They also asked people who have $0 invested in the stock market why they don't invest.

Here's the top reason that was given.

"I don't have enough wealth to invest in stocks"

If you don't invest at all—or you aren't investing as much as you could be—there's a good chance that this belief is holding you back.

---

16 https://news.gallup.com/poll/266807/percentage-americans-owns-stock.aspx

17 Choi, J. J., & Robertson, A. (2019, September 30). What Matters to Individual Investors? Evidence from the Horse's Mouth. Papers.ssrn.com. https://papers.ssrn.com/sol3/papers.cfm?abstract_id=3462048

Let's address the myth that investing is only for mustache-twirling rich guys with top hats and monocles.

It's never been easier to start small in the stock market

Many people think you need to pay big dollars in investment fees to advisors to start investing in the stock market.

That's simply not true.

In reality, It's never been easier for new investors with only a small amount of money to get started investing in the stock market.

There are a number of online brokerages that allow you to buy index funds for free—meaning they won't charge you a commission fee to execute the trade. Index funds allow you to buy the whole stock market for next to nothing. For example, the Management Expense Ratio for Vanguard's S&P 500 index fund is 0.03%. That means you pay about 3 cents per year for every $100 you invest.

So, you could start buying index funds without paying upfront fees and paying a fraction of a percentage point in annual investment fees. It's quite incredible when you think about it.

Another misconception that holds people back is that they don't believe they have enough money to invest to build any real wealth, so there's no point in bothering.

This kind of thinking is the easiest way to ensure you never build wealth.

Let's say you are 25 years old and start investing $25 per month and earn an annual return on investment of 6%. Even if you never increase your monthly investment contribution, **by the time you are 65, you will have $50,036.**

- $12,000 comes from your $25 monthly contributions.
- $38,036 comes from compounded interest.

If you waited until you were 35 to start investing, in order to end up with approximately $50,000 by the time you were 65, you would need to contribute $50 per month.

- $18,000 comes from your $25 monthly contributions and;
- $32,000 comes from compounded interest.

You still have $50,000, but since you waited 10 years to start contributing, you had to contribute 50% more of your own money to do so.

Time invested is the most important investing variable because it's the only variable you can control. Even if you only have $25 per month to invest, use time to your advantage.

Even more important than leveraging compound interest is the psychological benefit of going from *non-investor* to *investor*. Many people find the idea of investing their hard-earned money to be intimidating.

There is never a "*right time*" to start investing your money and taking control of your financial future. It's best to just "*rip the band-aid off*" as early on in life as possible.

In fact, it's much less scary to start investing $25 per month today than waiting 10 years from now and start investing $1,000 per month.

Let's say you invest $25 per month for a few years and have $500 invested in the market. Then the market gets cut in half, and your $500 becomes

$250. You just experienced the worst-case scenario that investors dread, and you are only down $250— which is unlikely to impact your financial stability. Since your paper loss is only a few hundred dollars, you might be less tempted to make a panic decision to sell and lock in a loss.

If you hold the course as a rational index investor, your investments will eventually recover and start growing your wealth gain. Learning these types of lessons when the amounts are small can benefit you greatly when the amount you have invested is significant.

Think of investing small amounts of money as your "*investing training wheels*". By the time you have a more substantial amount of money, you can invest every month. You will be an experienced investor and better prepared to handle the ups and downs of the stock market.

Start small, make it a habit, learn, master your emotions, and continue investing more down the road when you have more disposable income.

Part 2: The Alternatives to Index Investing

In Part 1, I reviewed the evidence and explained why low-cost, broad-based index funds are the rational investment to build passive wealth.

In Part 2, I will review the alternative investment products that the financial bullshitters will try and sell you on throughout your investing life. These alternatives will come with a sales pitch that will promise to "outperform" or "protect your downside". These are appeals to your greed and fear.

The rational investor pushes past greed and fear and makes decisions based on the best available evidence. In this chapter, I provide the evidence on each of these alternative investments to help you determine if they have a place in your portfolio.

Remember, portfolio allocation is a zero-sum game. Every dollar you allocate to alternative investments is a dollar not invested in passively managed index funds. If you are going to allocate money to an alternative investment ask yourself...given the risk, complexity and cost associated with this alternative investment, does it deserve a place in my portfolio over index funds?

Chapter 11: The Terrible Odds of Picking Stocks

It's not difficult to understand why so many people are drawn to the idea of investing in individual stocks in hopes of "*beating the market*". Picking stocks plays into several cognitive biases that humans suffer from, including overconfidence. Overconfidence is when people overestimate the probability of a good outcome and underestimate the probability of a bad outcome.

As I will demonstrate with data, anyone who picks stocks has an overconfidence bias. To be more specific, unless your name is Jim Simons or Warren Buffett, it is your portfolio that suffers from a stock-picking habit.

If you've made it to the eleventh chapter in a book about investing in index funds, you may be wondering, why would anyone bet their financial future on their ability to pick and choose individual stocks?

The same reason people go to the casino, it's fun, and they want to get rich quickly. In defense of anyone who picks stocks, the entire financial media ecosystem has been constructed to promote stock picking as a viable investment strategy for ordinary people.

If every blogger, investment newsletter, and TV show dedicated to the stock market told you the truth—your best bet is to buy a few index funds and sit on them for 20 plus years—they would quickly run out of business.

It's much easier to fill a 24/7 financial news cycle with stories about individual companies and whether you should buy, hold, or sell each of them than continue reporting that "yes, you should continue buying and holding index funds today."

Those who promote picking stocks are pushing a compelling story. That story is usually some variation of "If you listen to me, you too can become rich picking stocks." However, if you look at the data and academic research, it's clear that the story that stock pickers are pushing is simply that: a story.

The reality of picking stocks

Investing in the stock market is inherently riskier than investing in a safe asset such as short-term government bonds. Investors accept this increased risk because they are compensated with a higher expected return. The difference between the expected return of the stock market and risk-free assets is referred to as the risk premium for stocks.

If the stock market did not have a risk premium, there would be no incentive to invest in the stock market. Why take on more risk if you are not expecting higher returns? It's important to understand the two types of risk investors take on.

1. The risk that the entire stock market could drop is a systemic risk. Investors cannot diversify that risk away, but they are compensated with a risk premium.
2. The risk that an individual company or industry could collapse is called idiosyncratic risk. Investing in individual stocks presents an additional risk that investors aren't compensated for.

Translation: ***picking stocks introduces additional risk without increasing your expected return. There is no rational basis for investing this way.***

Much like the stock pickers, I just spun you a simple story about investing. Unlike the stock pickers, I will back up this story with academic research and data.

The Efficient Market Theory

We briefly touched on the efficient market theory in Chapter 4. If we accept that the stock market is efficient, it's reasonable to conclude that the most rational investment decision would be to invest in the entire stock market through low-cost index funds.

In a 1965 paper, the University of Chicago Economics Professor Eugene Fama concluded that stock market prices move randomly and that the price of stocks is representative of all known information.[18]

Put simply, Eugene Fama's research suggests that the stock market is reasonably efficient. In 2013, Fama won the Nobel Prize in Economics due to his research in this area. Fama's research would suggest that it's impossible for stock pickers to consistently beat the market. Stock pickers that do beat the market likely have done so due to luck rather than their brilliance and intuition.

The problem is that humans have a destructive habit of mistaking luck for skill. The more success you have, the more likely you are to believe that success is due to skill.

Numerous investment gurus called the financial crisis of 2008-2009 before it happened. This brought them fame and fortune and a standing invitation to appear on more financial TV shows. But when you take a closer look, you discover that these gurus are predicting a stock market crash every 18 months, and nine times out of ten, they are dead wrong.

---

18 Fama, E. F. (1965). Random Walks in Stock Market Prices. *Financial Analysts Journal, 21*(5), 55–59. https://doi.org/10.2469/faj.v21.n5.55

This is a perfect opportunity to remind everyone of a simple truth about decision-making: a bad decision (like picking stocks) can lead to a good outcome. That does not mean it was a good decision.

Let us now move to the data and evidence that suggests that picking stocks is, in fact, a bad decision.

Facts that stock pickers don't tell you

By picking individual stocks, you have a higher probability of underperforming a risk-free asset than beating the market.

If you currently own individual stocks, I urge you to read the 2018 paper by Hendrik Bessembinder from Arizona State University called, "Do Stocks Outperform Treasury Bills?"[19]

Here is a summary of the paper.

- Bessembinder studied the lifetime performance of individual stocks in the U.S. dating back to 1926.
- 60% of all stocks he studied had a lifetime return of less than a 30-day U.S. Treasury Bill (T-Bills).
- That means that you would have had better returns if you had invested in T-Bills (which are risk-free) than if you had invested in the majority of U.S. stocks since 1926.
- 4% of U.S. stocks accounted for 100% of the gains in the U.S. stock market since 1926.
- Bessembinder concluded that "The results help to explain why poorly-diversified active strategies most often underperform market averages."

19 Bessembinder, H. (2017). Do Stocks Outperform Treasury Bills? *SSRN Electronic Journal*. https://doi.org/10.2139/ssrn.2900447

The results of this research make it clear that picking stocks is a losing game. By picking individual stocks, you have a higher probability of underperforming a risk-free asset than you do of beating the market.

Stock pickers would tell you that all you need to do is find the 4% of stocks that drive the market, and you'll be rich. The problem is that there is no way of knowing which stocks will be part of that 4% that drive the market before they actually do it.

It's only in hindsight do we know which stocks moved the market.

It's easy to sit here today and conclude that the rise and dominance of a company like Apple was inevitable. But very few people were putting their money on Apple in 2002 when the stock was trading at 22 cents per share.

As legendary index investor and founder of Vanguard, Jack Bogle put it, "Don't look for the needle in the haystack. Just buy the haystack."

Translation: Don't invest in individual stocks. Invest in the entire market.

What's the worst that could happen?

The worst-case scenario for stock pickers is that the stock they pick goes to zero. While this is rare, it is not unheard of. Famous examples include Lehman Brothers and Enron.

While it is rare that you would lose "*all*" of your money picking stocks, it's not so rare to lose "*most*" of your money.

A 2014 study conducted by J.P. Morgan looked at all publicly traded stocks in the U.S. dating back to 1980. In the study, 40% of the 13,000 stocks declined by more than 70% from their peak value and never recovered.[20] Think of what would have to happen for an index fund that tracks the global stock market to fall 70% and never recover. The world would be in such shambles that what happens to your portfolio would be the least of your worries.

Taking on systematic risk is a bet that the world won't end, which is always a good bet because you either:

a.) Win that bet and make money or;

b.) You lose that bet, but the world ended, so who cares if you lost money?

Taking on idiosyncratic risk is a bet that an individual company will outperform the market. We just learned from looking at the data that when it comes to picking stocks, the most likely scenario is that you lose. That is a game I would rather not play.

---

20 *The Agony & The Ecstasy | J.P. Morgan Private Bank.* (n.d.). Privatebank.jpmorgan.com. Retrieved March 28, 2022, from https://privatebank.jpmorgan.com/gl/en/insights/investing/eotm/the-agony-the-ecstasy

Chapter 12:
The Basic Math of Actively Managed Mutual Funds

The paradoxical message of this book is that to be a great investor means being average.

In Chapter 11, we discussed the poor odds you'll face if you decide to pick and choose individual stocks. But what if, instead of picking stocks yourself, you paid some high-powered mutual fund managers on Wall Street to pick stocks for you? Would you expect to outperform my boring portfolio of index funds?

No.

The reality is that even the most brilliant investment managers on Wall Street fail to beat the market consistently. Even if they do outperform the market, most (or all) of that outperformance tends to get eaten up by the high fees of actively managed funds.

I'll prove it using basic math concepts most of us learn by the 5th grade.

The arithmetic of active management

At the time I write this, over the past 10 years, 83% of actively managed investment funds in the U.S underperformed the S&P 500[21] when investment fees are taken into account.

That should tell you all you need to know about the paradox of investing. The only reason someone would pay higher fees for an actively managed mutual fund—when they could stick their money in an index fund for

21 *PIVA | S&P Dow Jones Indices*. (n.d.). Www.spglobal.com. Retrieved March 28, 2022, from https://www.spglobal.com/spdji/en/research-insights/spiva/

next to nothing—is because they expect the fund manager to outperform the index.

Actively managed mutual funds try really hard to deliver higher than average returns. They hire brilliant investment managers and an army of analysts who spend all day looking for investment opportunities to exploit. For all of their efforts and resources, they fail to beat boring old index funds the vast majority of the time.

William Sharpe explains why most active managers fail to deliver so-called "alpha" (higher risk-adjusted returns than the market) in his 1991 paper, "The Arithmetic of Active Management".[22]

As Sharpe says, the case for investing in actively managed mutual funds only makes sense if you are willing to suspend the laws of basic arithmetic.

Here are a few basic facts you need to understand before we break down the grade-school math on why mutual funds are not a rational choice.

- Actively managed funds have higher fees (often 1%-2% per year) than passively managed index funds (often below 0.1% per year).
- Remember, an index fund replicates the stock market. If Amazon is 4% of the S&P 500, it will make up 4% of an S&P 500 index fund.
- So, an index fund will provide investors with the average market return minus its nominal fee.

22 Sharpe, W. F. (1991). The Arithmetic of Active Management. *Financial Analysts Journal, 47*(1), 7-9. https://doi.org/10.2469/faj.v47.n1.7

- Actively managed mutual funds pay a portfolio manager to make investment decisions. If the manager believes Amazon's stock will fall, they will hold less Amazon stock than the index fund.

The following quote from Sharpe is also critical to understand, so I will break it into two parts.

> *"Before costs, the return on the average actively managed dollar will be equal to the return on the average passively managed dollar."*

When you add up the returns of all of the actively managed investments in the stock market, you get, well, the stock market. So mathematically, it must be true that the average actively managed dollar is equal to the average market return before we account for investment fees.

Here's another quote from Sharpe in his 1991 paper.

> *"After costs, the return on the actively managed dollar will be less than the return on the passively managed dollar."*

Which is exactly what we see in the data. 83% of actively managed U.S. investment funds underperform the S&P 500 when accounting for investment fees.

If the average return between index funds and mutual funds are the same, but index funds have much lower fees, then the net return of index funds > actively managed mutual funds.

A common marketing talking point made by the financial services industry is that active management works better in international markets where local stock markets are "less efficient" than the U.S. market and therefore provide active managers with better odds of outperforming.

The data tells a different story.

At the time I write this, over the past 10 years:

- 83% of European active managers have underperformed the S&P Europe 350.
- 83% of Canadian active managers have underperformed the TSX.
- 86% of Mexican active managers have underperformed the S&P/ BMV IRT.
- 87% of Brazilian active managers have underperformed the S&P Brazil BMI.
- 79% of Japanese active managers have underperformed the S&P/ TOPIX 150.
- 84% of Australian active managers have underperformed the S&P/ ASX 200.
- 83% of Indian active managers have underperformed the S&P BSE 100.

There is no evidence to suggest actively managed mutual funds perform any better internationally than they do in the U.S.

I discuss this issue of active vs. passive investing a lot on my blog.[23] When I present this data to readers, the most common pushback I receive is, "Ben, you're talking about the average mutual fund, but I would never invest in an average mutual fund. "

Let's dig a little deeper and understand why it's so incredibly difficult to:

1. Outperform the stock market consistently over a long period of time.
2. Pick an investment manager that will consistently outperform before they actually do it.

23 Le Fort, B. (n.d.). *Making of a Millionaire.* Benlefort.substack.com. Retrieved March 28, 2022, from https://benlefort.substack.com/

The crowding out of skilled active managers

A 2014 paper published in the Journal of Financial Economics explains in simple terms why it's becoming increasingly difficult for any investment manager to consistently outperform the market.[24]

Put simply: there are too many skilled investors in the market today.

The bulk of stocks are owned by institutional investors, think Vanguard, BlackRock, pension funds, and endowments. These institutions hire brilliant people to manage their portfolios. Anytime a stock is bought or sold, there is an excellent chance that the person on either side of that trade is highly skilled.

Remember, when you buy a stock, it means someone else is selling it. They are selling it because they have the opposite prediction about where the price of that stock is going. You are buying because you think the price is going up, and the other person is selling because they believe the price is going down.

If the bulk of the stock market involved trades between amateurs, it would be much easier for skilled investment managers to find inefficiencies and generate alpha.

But when the Harvard endowment investment manager chooses to sell a stock to a hedge fund manager, these two managers are more equally matched. This means the more trades between skilled managers, the more even the split will be between who wins those trades.

24 Pastor, L., Stambaugh, R. F., & Taylor, L. (2013). Scale and Skill in Active Management. *SSRN Electronic Journal.* https://doi.org/10.2139/ssrn.2318788

As more and more assets are controlled by large institutional investors who hire the most brilliant managers, there is a smaller chance that these brilliant managers can generate alpha because they are squaring off against equally brilliant managers.

So, as we see in the real world data, most active managers will return about the market average before fees.

Either way, the best you can expect is to earn the average market return. This leads us to the obvious conclusion that the most important investment factor in our control is investment fees. This leads us to another obvious conclusion that low-cost index funds are the rational investment choice over actively managed mutual funds.

Chapter 13: Even More Evidence in Favor of Passive as Opposed to Active Funds

A 2014 study by Richard Ferri and Alex Benke wanted to test how real-life portfolios of actual index and actively managed funds performed against each other over time.[25]

This study differs from most studies of actively managed funds vs. the benchmark index for two reasons.

1. Rather than comparing an active fund to the index, they compare it to an equivalent index fund from Vanguard.
2. The study addressed the issue of survivorship bias.

Survivorship bias artificially inflates the perceived performance of actively managed investment funds by excluding funds that have gone out of business or merged with other funds.

You might be surprised by how many active funds end up closing shop. A research paper by Vanguard titled "The mutual fund graveyard: An analysis of dead funds" found that 46% of mutual funds that were available in 1997 no longer existed by 2011.[26]

---

25 Ferri, R., & Benke, A. (2014). *A Case for Index Fund Portfolios* [Review of *A Case for Index Fund Portfolios*].

26 Schlanger, T., & Philips, C. (n.d.). *The mutual fund graveyard: An analysis of dead funds*. Retrieved May 14, 2022, from https://www.devriesinvestmentservices.nl/images/stories/home/Downloads/ICRMFG_012013_MFGraveyard.pdf

In a surprise to no one, these funds that go out of business tend to perform very poorly in the years leading up to their demise. Including these dead funds in this type of analysis is useful because it is more representative of what happens in real life.

The portfolios

While the study ran through six-different scenarios of different passive and active portfolios, I will focus on scenario one for two reasons:

1. All the scenarios draw a similar conclusion (index funds outperforming).
2. It uses one of the most popular portfolio constructions: 60% stocks and 40% bonds, often referred to as the 60/40 portfolio.

It's important to note that the 60% stocks portion was two made up of 40% U.S. stocks and 20% international, while the 40% of bonds were made up entirely of U.S. investment-grade bonds.

Ferri and Benke ran 5,000 permutations of active funds and were compared to three Vanguard index funds that meet the 60/40 portfolio definition from 1997–2012.

It's important to note that this timeline includes the dot com bubble and the great financial crisis of 2007-2009.

One of the arguments for active management is that they can "protect your downside" in the event of a stock market crash. If this is true, we would expect the active managers to perform well during this volatile investment period.

Except that didn't happen.

It was never close

The index fund portfolio outperformed the randomly selected actively managed fund portfolios 83% of the time.

To be exact:

- 4,144 of the active fund portfolios underperformed the index portfolio. These funds underperformed the index portfolio by 1.25% per year on average.
- 856 of the active fund portfolios outperformed the index portfolio. These funds outperformed by 0.52% per year on average.

Takeaways

Here are two clear takeaways for investors.

1. There was little evidence of active managers "protecting your downside" as 83% of actively managed 60/40 portfolios underperformed through a time period that included two of the biggest stock market crashes on record.
2. Another argument of active managers is that even though they underperform on average when they do outperform, they do so by a wide margin. The evidence suggests that not only is that incorrect, but the opposite was true for this sample: when index portfolios outperformed—which was 83% of the time—they did so by a much wider margin (1.25%) than when active portfolios outperformed (0.52%)

Here's a two-sentence summary of these results.

The index portfolios clobbered the active portfolios. If this was a little league game, they would have enacted the mercy rule and stopped the game.

Chapter 14: Beware of Index Funds in Name Only

At this point in our journey together, I hope you agree that passively managed index funds are the rational way to invest in the stock market.

The problem is that there are real index funds and fake index funds. The real index funds have one job, and they do it great: track a stock market index like the S&P 500. Fake index funds market themselves as "passive" investments, but in reality, they are nothing more than closeted active funds and, therefore, should surprise no one that they underperform.

Let's dig into how you can spot a fake index fund and why you should avoid them.

We are drowning in an ocean of ETFs

According to Statista, there were 7,602 Exchange Traded Funds (ETFs) in 2019.[27]

In Chapter 4, we discussed that although the terms are often used interchangeably, not all ETFs are index funds.

Index funds are defined by their passive investment strategy of replicating a particular index of assets.

---

27 Number of ETFs worldwide 2019. (n.d.). Statista. https://www.statista.com/statistics/278249/global-number-of-etfs/

ETFs are defined as a specific structure of an investment fund that is easy for DIY investors to trade.

I'll say it one last time. Not all Index funds are ETFs, and not all ETFs are index funds.

Many index funds are not ETFs but are structured as traditional mutual funds. This means they are not bought on stock exchanges but directly through investment fund companies.

Many ETFs do not follow an indexing strategy. This means active fund managers pick and choose assets rather than follow a passive investment strategy.

Of those 7,602 ETFs, only a tiny portion of those would market themselves as index funds. Of the subset of index funds that market themselves as "passive", 1/3 are what we would call closet active management funds. That means they present themselves as passive index funds, but they are actually actively managed.

Let's examine evidence from a 2021 paper titled "Closet Active Management of Passive Funds".[28] The researchers examined prospectus data (the details of each fund) to determine if each so-called passive index fund performed the only task of a truly passive index fund: to track the performance of a broad-based stock market index like the S&P 500 or the MSCI World Index.

28 Akey, P., Robertson, A., & Simutin, M. (2021). Closet active management of passive funds. SSRN Electronic Journal. https://doi.org/10.2139/ssrn.3874582

They found that 1/3 of these "passive" investments are little more than actively managed funds with better marketing.

The two common tells of closeted active funds

The researchers found two ways in which these funds employed active management.

First, the weighting of their holdings was often not in line with the index they were supposed to track.

By going through the fund prospectus, the researchers uncovered the active investment strategies being deployed. Remember, for a "real" passively managed index fund; there is a single strategy: replicate the returns of the underlying index. Any investment funds that do anything more can no longer be considered "passive."

Second, many index funds use a proprietary index developed or purchased by the fund company.

This point is critical because it highlights that even if an investment tracks an underlying index, that does not guarantee it's a passive investment.

Investment fund companies can build their own "index" and create their own rules to determine how the index of investments is constructed. In doing so, they are making the active decision of what assets get included.

There's nothing stopping a fund company from constructing a dog-food index that tracks the performance of all the companies that make dog food. Technically speaking, that would be considered an "index fund".

Contrast that to truly passive index funds that try to replicate an entire stock market rather than one sub-sector like dog food.

Closeted active funds underperform real index funds

The unsurprising result from the research is that these closeted active funds (masquerading as passive investments) underperform truly passive index funds that track broad-based indices.

For funds with a high tracking error for the index they track: a one standard deviation in "Active Weight" (a measure of how active the fund manager is) is associated with a 0.55% decrease in annual returns.

For funds that use a proprietary index: A one standard deviation in "Active Weight" is associated with a 0.95% decrease in annual returns.

The opportunity cost of investing in closeted active funds grows over time.

If you invested $10,000 in a passively managed index fund that returned 8% per year after 30 years, you would have $100,627.

If you invested $10,000 in a closeted active fund, you would have between $77,197 and $86,336 after 30 years based on the average underperformance of these types of funds.

The opportunity cost of closeted active funds in this example would be $14,291-$23,430. This equals a 14%-23% loss of wealth over 30 years.

That is a meaningful amount of money.

This highlights the importance of understanding what you are investing in. If you want to invest in passive index funds, it's important to look at the investment prospectus to see what the investment strategy is and what index this fund is tracking.

If you take one lesson from this chapter, let it be this. Truly passive index funds have one job: to the extent possible, track the performance of an underlying broad-based index. Think the S&P 500, not the proprietary dog-food index.

Chapter 15: Thematic ETFs are an Expensive Way to Express Your Worldview

Don't let your money die so you can express your beliefs.

That's what most investors do when they buy so-called "thematic" ETFs.

Thematic investing is a bit of a squishy term but generally refers to a fund that invests in companies that some think will benefit from societal and technological shifts. Environmental, social, and corporate governance or "ESG" is one form of thematic investing, but there are many other thematic ETFs out there.

- Weed stocks
- Blockchain
- "Disruptive" technologies
- "Social sentiment" aka meme stocks

If an issue is trending on Twitter, you can probably find a fund company willing to wrap that issue into an ETF and sell it to you.

Thematic ETFs are a great business model for fund companies but often lead to bad outcomes for investors. To find out why let's examine the evidence and apply basic logic to thematic investing.

Thematic ETFs are popular because they appeal to passion rather than reason

Here's the basic pitch of most thematic investment funds: "Hey, you know that societal issue you care deeply about or that technology you believe will change the world? Give us your money, and we'll invest in it."

To be honest, it's a pretty genius sales pitch. Why wouldn't you want to align your money with your values?

Here's one reason why: you'll likely lose money, which means you'll have less resources to dedicate to that cause you care about in the future.

Excitement and investing make a dangerous cocktail

Here's a rule of thumb you might find helpful.

If you're excited about what you're investing in, odds are it's a bad investment.

The more excited you are about the companies you are investing in, the less likely you are to care about things like the earnings and debt loads of those companies.

An investor who buys an ESG fund wants to "feel good" about aligning their money with issues they care about, like green energy and social equality. If that's your primary motivation as an investor, you're likely to overpay to buy assets that make you feel good.

The dreadful performance of thematic ETFs is captured perfectly in a 2021 paper titled "Competition for Attention in the ETF Space" written by Ben-David et al.[29] In this paper, the researchers lay out the scenario in which most thematic ETFs are created.

- A particular technology or societal issue gains momentum in the public consciousness.
- Right around the time excitement for that issue peaks, a thematic ETF is launched.

---

29 Ben-David, I., Franzoni, F. A., Kim, B., & Moussawi, R. (2021). Competition for Attention in the ETF Space. SSRN Electronic Journal. https://doi.org/10.2139/ssrn.3772608

- Given the excitement for this new trend, valuations of the companies within the thematic fund often peak in a similar timeframe.
- Money pours into the thematic funds, further driving up valuations.
- Eventually, the excitement wears off, and stock prices come tumbling back to reality.

The researchers found specialized ETFs lose 30% of their risk-adjusted value within five years of the ETF launching, on average. They found that this underperformance was not driven by fees (which are high) but by the overvaluation of the stocks within the fund.

Here's the quote from the Ben-David et al. paper that brings it all together.

> "*Overall, providers appear to cater to investors' extrapolative beliefs by issuing specialized ETFs that track attention-grabbing themes.*"

An example of thematic investing gone wrong: Canadian Weed stocks

Canadian weed is the perfect example of the excitement bubble of thematic ETFs.

- In 2017, the North American Marijuana Index was created. The index tracks the performance of publically traded companies active in the marijuana industry.
- In 2018, Canada legalized recreational marijuana.
- Investors got excited, and a number of thematic ETFs grew up from the ground that invested in companies selling legal weed.
- After legalization, The North American Marijuana Index increased by 150% within a few months in the fall of 2018—the point at which many excited investors jumped on the bandwagon.

- Companies selling legal weed saw their valuations skyrocket. After all, weed is a "growth industry".
- After an extremely volatile year, the market for legal weed companies peaked in late 2019.
- At the time I write this in May 2022, the North American Marijuana Index is down 77% from its 2019 peak and is actually lower than before weed became legal in Canada.

This isn't such a bad deal for thematic ETF providers. They get to charge high investment fees and profit off catering to investors' irrational belief that because something is "good" or "exciting" it will be a good investment.

If things don't work out, you create a new ETF based on the latest trending issue, collect more fees and rinse and repeat.

For the investor, it's a double kick in the pants. Losing money is never fun, but losing money betting on an issue that you care deeply about creates an added level of psychological pain.

The people who have the capacity to effect the most change are the wealthy. Wealthy people have financial resources and time to dedicate to causes they care about.

Rather than gambling your money on thematic ETFs, invest in a simple portfolio of index funds. If you want to contribute to a cause, start by contributing your time. Then as you keep investing in index funds and your wealth grows over time, you can afford to give more money to the causes you care about.

Chapter 16:
Dividends Feel Like "Free Money", but They're not

The rational investor cares about one thing: total investment returns.

Total returns for stock market investors = capital gains + dividends - investment fees & taxes

All that matters is, what is my account balance? If you have a $100,000 portfolio, the $100,000 is all we should care about. We shouldn't care whether that $100,000 came from dividends or capital gains (increase in share prices).

Except most people care. They care a lot.

Investors love using dividends to buy stuff

A 2021 paper titled "Consuming Dividends" written by Konstantin Bräuer (University of Frankfurt), Andreas Hackethal (University of Frankfurt), and Tobin Hanspal (Vienna University) examined why investors are drawn to dividend-paying stocks and how some investors plan their entire financial life around dividends.[30]

The researchers used bank data, portfolio data, and survey data to measure how investors' spending habits changed around days of receiving dividend income from a portfolio. Their findings show that many investors allowed their spending to be dictated by the dividend policies of the companies they invest in.

---

30 Bräuer, K., Hackethal, A., & Hanspal, T. (2019). Consuming Dividends. *SSRN Electronic Journal.* https://doi.org/10.2139/ssrn.3466731

Finding #1: Investors are significantly more comfortable spending dividends than their paycheck.

- 14.4% of dividends an investor receives are spent on one-off purchases within a week. The majority of that spending occurred on the day they received the dividend.
- Only 9.6% of labor income was spent on similar purchases within the same period.

Finding #2: Dividend bias exists for the young and old and the rich and not-so-rich.

- Increased consumption around dividend payments is significant across wealth and age distributions.

Finding #3: Supersavers are the most reliant on dividends to fuel their spending

- Past research has suggested that those who rely on dividends lack self-control in their spending habits.
- This study finds the opposite result: "those who would prefer to save rather than spend, consume a larger fraction of their dividend income precisely around days of its arrival.
- Those who actively plan their finances consume a much greater share of dividends they receive compared to those who don't have a financial plan. This finding suggests that investors intentionally rely on dividends to pay for their cost of living as a key pillar in their financial plan.

Finding #4: 61% of respondents view dividends as expected income like a salary or work bonus.

- Investors who think of dividends as expected money spend a greater proportion of the dividends they receive.

Here's a simplified summary of these findings: People tend to feel extremely comfortable spending dividend money, even more than spending money from their paycheck. This is not an accident but a central component of their financial plan to pay for their cost of living with dividend income.

Dividends feel like "free money", but they're not

To the rational investor, it doesn't matter if returns come from capital gains, dividends, or some combination of the two.

If you want to buy tickets for a concert that add up to $500, the tickets will still cost you $500 of your portfolio whether you choose to make the purchase using dividends or by selling a few shares and using capital gains.

Income is income.

However, most investors are not rational, and they have a firewall in their minds that separates dividends from capital gains.

- Dividends are viewed as "real" money that can be spent.
- Capital gains are viewed as "temporary" money that should not be touched.

The real reason we prefer to spend dividends and sit on capital gains is that we are afraid that selling shares to fuel consumption will lead to a situation where we run out of money. The dividend investor feels safe because they are not "touching their principal".

This type of thinking is a fallacy.

When companies issue dividends, the value of the company goes down. A mathematical fact that even sophisticated investors ignore.

If a company is holding $100 million in cash from profits, it has two options.

1. Retain the $100 million.
2. Payout $100 million in dividends.

If the company pays out the $100 million in dividends, it just gave away $100 million in assets, and—all else being equal— the value of the company falls by $100 million. It's basic math that dividend investors choose to ignore.

This reality is expertly explained in a 2018 paper titled "The Dividend Disconnect", in which authors Samuel Hartzmark (University of Chicago) and David Solomon (Boston College) examine the reasons investors have a disconnect between dividends and capital gains.[31]

Hartzmark and Solomon refer to the popular (and incorrect) perception that dividends are stable and secure in times when the stock market is crashing as "the free dividends fallacy".

The primary reason for the widespread belief in the free dividend fallacy is that the price of stocks is extremely visible and easy to access. You can

31 Hartzmark, S. M. (2016). The Dividend Disconnect. SSRN Electronic Journal. https://doi.org/10.2139/ssrn.2876373

open your phone and see the change in the price of a stock second by second. Most investors only find out about a change in a company's dividend policy when a press release is issued (that the investor probably won't read) or when the dividend payment they receive is suddenly smaller than what they expected.

The downside of dividend investing

So far, we have covered why investors love dividends (they wrongfully view it as free money) and why—all else being equal— the rational investor is indifferent between dividends and capital gains.

Let's conclude our discussion on dividend investing by acknowledging two factors that prevent rational investors from focusing on dividend-paying stocks:

1. Dividends reduce total returns.
2. Focusing on dividends reduces the diversification of your portfolio.

How dividend investing can hurt your ability to accumulate wealth

If you invest in a tax-sheltered retirement account, like an IRA in the U.S, or an RRSP in Canada, you should be indifferent to whether or not you receive dividends.

If you are investing in a taxable account, dividends will trigger additional taxes and reduce your net investment returns. If an investor receives $10,000 in dividends, they must pay tax on that $10,000. If the share price increases by $10,000 but no dividends are issued, no tax is payable.

Receiving dividends at times when you don't need the income will lead to unnecessary tax bills.

Remember, total returns = capital gains + dividends - investment fees & taxes

The positive impact of receiving a dividend is partially offset by an increase in taxes.

If an investor is selling shares to create income, they can control when this tax is paid by choosing when they want to sell their shares.

By waiting to sell their shares in a year where their income is low, either in retirement or in a year when they have lost their job, they will pay less tax than the dividend investor who receives dividends during their high-income years.

There is an additional downside to receiving dividends which is that—as I've already pointed out— investors are more likely to spend their dividends rather than reinvest them. Failing to reinvest dividends (thinking they are free money) will greatly reduce lifetime wealth accumulation.

Dividend focused portfolios are under-diversified

The number of stocks in the global market that pay dividends has been steadily declining for decades.[32]

- In 1991, 71% of global stocks paid dividends.
- By 2012, only 61% of global stocks paid dividends.

32 *Global Dividend-Paying Stocks: A Recent History*. (2013). https://www.pwlcapital.com/wp-content/uploads/2019/04/Dimensional-global_dividends_white_paper.pdf

Focusing exclusively on stocks that pay dividends means you are excluding 40% of the global stock market from your portfolio.

Dividend investors are making an inherit bet that dividend investing stocks will outperform the market moving forward. There is no evidence to suggest this is the case.

It's important to remember why diversification is so important. Put simply, it maximizes your probability of a successful investment outcome.

The dividend fallacy—believing that dividends are free money—is one of the most common mistakes investors make.

In reality, dividends are not "free money". Dividends are an inflexible, tax-inefficient way to receive investment income while reducing the diversification in a portfolio.

The rational investor focuses less on passive income (dividends) and more on passive wealth (capital gains + dividends).

Chapter 17:
How Real Estate Fits Into a Portfolio

Confession time.

Stocks are not the asset class with the highest risk-adjusted returns. That honor belongs to real estate.

That was the finding of a 2017 paper titled "The Rate of Return on Everything, 1870-2015", written by researchers from the Federal Reserve Bank of San Francisco.[33] **Over the 130-year sample, they found the global stock market provided real returns of 6.89% per year compared to 7.05% for global real estate**. Not only did real estate provide better returns, it did so with significantly less volatility.

Global real estate has provided superior returns, and the ride has been significantly less bumpy.

You might be wondering if this book is a guide to rational investing, why isn't it focused on the asset class that has provided the highest risk-adjusted returns?

It's a fair question. The answer is that real estate is a complicated asset class and the findings of the Federal Reserve paper come with important caveats.

Let's dive into those complications and caveats and explore how real estate fits into a portfolio.

33 Jordà, Ò., Knoll, K., Kuvshinov, D., Schularick, M., & Taylor, A. M. (2018). The Rate of Return on Everything, 1870-2015. SSRN Electronic Journal. https://doi.org/10.2139/ssrn.3164778

Homeownership vs. real estate investing

The first and most important complication we must address when discussing investing in real estate is "What does investing in real estate mean to you?"

There are two very different ways people invest in real estate.

1. Owning a home
2. Buying investment properties

Homeownership as an investment

The most important caveat you need to know is that 7.05% annual return for real estate does not apply to owner-occupied housing.

There are two ways to make money in real estate.

1. Collecting rent.
2. The value of the property increases.

You don't collect rent when you own a home and live in it, and roughly half of that 7.05% return disappears. The house you live in is not a better investment than stocks, let's get that out of the way.

Here are a few other points that make owning a home a less attractive investment compared to investing in stocks through index funds.

Owning a home is the ultimate idiosyncratic risk

In Chapter 4, I introduced the concept of idiosyncratic risk, which in the context of picking stocks is a risk that is unique to an individual company. Owning a home is as idiosyncratic as an investment can get.

Buying a home means buying a single unit of:

- A broad asset class: real estate.
- A subsector of real estate: single-family homes.
- Single-family home in a particular country.
- Single-family home in a particular state or province within that country.
- Single-family home in a particular city within that state or province.
- Single-family home in a particular neighborhood within that city.
- Single-family home on a particular street within that neighborhood.

In real estate, they say the most important factor is "location, location, location", which is 100% accurate. Every real estate market is unique. The factors that impact the value of a home in Detroit, Michigan, are radically different than what impacts the value of a home in London, England.

Homes are riskier than you think

Before the financial crisis, nearly everyone believed that it was a fact of life that house prices in America would always go up every year. While the events of 2008-2009 disproved that belief, houses are still considered a safe investment.

That belief is backed up by the research from the Federal Reserve, which found the volatility of global real estate returns was roughly half the standard deviation for global stocks.

What we can take from that is that owning a home will have less price volatility than a 100% equity portfolio. But remember, putting 100% of your money in stocks is very aggressive and risky. Housing being less risky than a 100% stock portfolio does not make it "safe".

Government bonds are "safe", but buying a house involves risk.

The question is, how much risk?

That question was answered in a 2017 paper titled "The Home as a Risky Asset", written by David Blanchett published in the Journal of Personal Finance.[34] Blanchett found that owning a home was equally as risky as a 60/40 portfolio of stocks and government bonds.

He also concluded that the realized returns of homeowners are often less than inflation when you account for maintenance costs, taxes, and transaction fees. This is especially true for homeowners who move a lot.

A paid-off house provides risk-free income

I don't want to give you the idea that owning a home is a bad idea, you just shouldn't count on your home to be your primary means of accumulating wealth. But there are a lot of benefits of owning a home.

If you bought your home using a mortgage, it creates forced savings. Every time you make a mortgage payment a portion of that payment goes towards paying down the principal of the loan—which makes you a little bit richer.

Nearly every developed country in the world provides major tax incentives to homeowners. For example, Americans can deduct a portion of their mortgage interest against their income. Canadians don't have to pay any capital gains taxes when they sell their primary residence. These tax incentives make homeownership an effective vehicle in which to accumulate personal wealth.

34 Blanchett, D. (2017). The Home as a Risky Asset [Review of The Home as a Risky Asset]. Journal of Personal Finance.

The largest benefit of homeownership is very subtle but very powerful.

Homeownership acts as a form of rent control.

If you have a fixed-rate mortgage, your housing costs on a year-to-year basis will be relatively flat. You are not subject to the landlord jacking up your rent when market conditions allow them to do so. If you can continue increasing your income throughout your career, having a fixed-rate mortgage means that your housing costs as a percentage of your income will drop on a year-over-year basis.

As housing costs as a percentage of your income drop, that frees up more money that you can invest in index funds and build passive wealth.

Once the mortgage is paid off, your housing costs drop to the level of your property taxes and local maintenance costs.

A paid-off mortgage is like receiving tax-free income from a bond. If your mortgage payment was $1,500, paying off that mortgage is no different than receiving $1,500 per month in tax-free and risk-free income. That not only frees up more money for you to invest, but all else being equal, a paid-off mortgage increases your capacity to be more aggressive in your investment portfolio.

Rental properties as an investment

Buying a house and renting it out is a completely different investment than buying a house to live in yourself.

Rental properties are the investment that has historically provided a 7.05% annual real return. So does that mean you should sell your index funds and go buy rental properties?

No.

If you are self-managing your real estate portfolio, you don't have a passive investment; you have a business. Your return on investment with rental properties is directly linked to your skill at finding deals, finding tenants, and managing the property. Rental properties can be incredible wealth-building assets, but only if you are a skilled real estate investor. If you make terrible decisions, you could lose your shirt in real estate.

For some people investing in real estate will lead to financial freedom, but for others, it could lead to financial ruin.

Compare that to investing in a globally diversified index fund; you invest and do nothing. Getting paid to do nothing, that's how you build passive wealth. They will never make a reality show about index investors like they do with real estate, but the boring, rational approach works.

There is another very big caveat you need to be aware of with the annual returns of real estate. That 7.05% annual return does not account for property taxes. A rule of thumb is that property taxes are roughly 1% of the value of a property. Including property taxes drops the net return on real estate to 6.05%, which is less than stocks.

Another important caveat is that to capture that ~~7.05%~~ 6.05% real return, an investor would have needed to have bought investment properties in all 16 countries that the Federal Reserve researchers included in their study.

Given the price of a single property and the high transaction fees involved in buying real estate, it would be nearly impossible for individual investors to build a globally diversified portfolio of rental properties across 16 countries. In contrast, the rational investor can buy a single index fund that tracks the global stock market with a few clicks.

Finally, real estate as an investment has another drawback: lack of liquidity.

If you own a rental property worth $500,000, you can't decide to sell $100,000 worth of the property. It's an all-or-nothing proposition. If you decided to sell the entire property, it would take weeks or months and costs thousands of dollars. If you have $500,000 in index funds, you can quickly sell $100,000 in a matter of seconds at a minimal cost.

There is one way that individual investors can invest in global real estate as easily as investors who invest in the stock market. We will discuss how in the next chapter.

Chapter 18:
REITs: A Rational Way to Invest in Real Estate?

In Chapter 17, I highlighted three problems with real estate investing:

1. Lack of diversification.
2. Large financial and time commitments are required to manage properties.
3. Lack of liquidity.

What if I told you that you could invest in real estate and diversify over thousands of properties, and you would never have to think about fixing a leaky toilet?

You can do that by investing in Real Estate Investment Trusts (REITs).

Do REITs have a place in the portfolio of a rational investor? Let's have a look at the evidence.

What is a REIT?

REITs are companies that invest in commercial real estate. REITs invest in a variety of Real Estate projects that most regular people would not have the capital to invest in, such as:

- Large apartment complexes
- Office buildings
- Healthcare facilities
- Retirement facilities
- Shopping malls
- Retail plazas

- Industrial buildings
- Factories, warehouses, and other industrial buildings

Public REITs are traded on the stock exchange, where investors can purchase shares in the same way you would buy shares of Apple, Amazon, or any other publicly-traded company.

While they are publicly traded the same as any other stock, REITs have unique characteristics that make them different from many other stocks.

The first and most obvious difference is that REITs only invest in real estate assets.

The most crucial difference between REITs and other stocks is their distribution requirements. REITs in the United States are required to pay 90% of their taxable income in the form of shareholder distributions each year. This is in stark contrast to traditional stocks, which are free to set their dividend payout policy however they see fit.

REITs have historically provided excellent total returns

In Chapter 16, I reviewed the evidence why rational investors don't chase dividends: they focus on total returns.

REITs have historically provided strong total returns.

From 1972 to 2019, the S&P 500 provided investors a total annual return of 12.1% compared to total returns of 13.3% for the FTSE NAREIT index of U.S. equity REITs.[35]

---

35 DiLallo, M. (2020, August 5). REITs vs. Stocks: What Does the Data Say? The Motley Fool. https://www.fool.com/research/reits-vs-stocks/

Amazingly, the historical total returns on REITs have outperformed the general stock market. What is even better is that since these asset classes have had a low correlation, meaning their prices do not always move in the same direction or magnitude, there appears to be a diversification benefit of adding REITs to a portfolio.

Do you need REITs in your portfolio?

Given their unique characteristics and imperfect correlation with the broad stock market, investors often view REITs as a district asset class that deserves an allocation in a properly diversified portfolio of stocks and bonds.

In a 2017 paper, Jared Kizer and Sean Grover answered the question, "Are REITs a Distinct Asset Class?"[36]

To answer that question, Kizer and Grover established four characteristics of a unique asset class.

1. Low correlation with established asset classes such as stocks and bonds.
2. Statistically significant outperformance with respect to generally accepted factor models.
3. Inability to be replicated, on a co-movement basis, by a long-only portfolio holding established asset classes
4. Improved risk-adjusted returns when added to a portfolio holding established asset classes.

They found that REITs failed to distinguish themselves on all four criteria as a distinct asset class.

36 Kizer, J., & Grover, S. (2017). Are REITs a Distinct Asset Class? SSRN Electronic Journal. https://doi.org/10.2139/ssrn.2965146

A 2018 paper written by Peter Mladina published in the Journal of Investing came to the same conclusion: REITs are not a distinct asset class materially different from stocks.[37] Mladina found that the risk-return profile of REITs resembled a portfolio of 60% small-cap value stocks and 40% high-yield bonds. We can achieve the same risk-adjusted returns that REITs provide through a diversified portfolio of stocks and bonds.

Finally, we must consider that REITs only invest in real estate, which means they are exposed to idiosyncratic risks specific to the real estate sector. Think of what happened in 2020, the COVID-19 pandemic hammered REITs that invest in retail and office buildings.

Retail and office REITs make up a large portion of the REIT index. If you over-allocate to REITs, you have to worry if work-from-home policies or the rise of online shopping will permanently damage your portfolio. This is not something you have to worry about if you invest in a globally diversified portfolio of broad-based index funds.

As Kizer and Grover point out, REITs make up about 2.5% of the U.S. stock market. If you are an index investor, you already have a portion of your portfolio allocated to REITs; you just don't realize it.

Given the results of Kizer and Grover and Mladina, there is no rationale for allocating any more of your portfolio to REITs.

Using REITs to keep your real estate bias in check

The rational investor looks at the evidence and decides there is no reason to overweight REITs in their portfolio.

---

37 Mladina, P. (2018). Real Estate Betas and the Implications for Asset Allocation. *The Journal of Investing, 27*(1), 109–120. https://doi.org/10.3905/joi.2018.27.1.109

However, most people have a strong bias toward real estate. It's difficult to resist the urge to invest in real estate when hundreds of reality TV shows make real estate investing look easy, fun, and profitable.

I am no different.

As the son of two real estate agents, I have a deeply embedded bias toward real estate. To keep that bias in check, I dedicate a small portion of my portfolio to overweighting REITs.

It is a small allocation, I buy REIT index ETFs rather than individual REITs, and I only keep REITs in tax-sheltered accounts.

The rational choice would be to forget about REITs and stick to a pure broad-based index fund strategy. But, if a small overweighting towards REITs allows you to scratch that "real estate itch" without going $700,000 in debt to buy a single rental property, it can be well worth it.

Chapter 19: Preferred Shares Look Like a Stock and Act Like a Bond

At some point in your investing journey, you will be pitched on investing in so-called "alternative" assets. These investments are pitched as an alternative to the traditional portfolio of stocks and bonds.

A popular alternative asset often pitched to income-hungry investors during times of low interest rates and yields is "preferred shares", which are a hybrid asset that falls somewhere between a stock and a bond.

Let's explore some of the basic features of preferred shares, how they are similar and different from stocks and bonds, and highlight some of the risks involved.

What are preferred shares?

Preferred shares are a hybrid investment that shares features of bonds and some features of common stocks (common stocks being the type of stock found in a total market index fund).

If you take one thing away from this chapter, let it be this: Preferred shares are a complex investment.

Not all preferred shares are created equal; there different types of preferred shares that each have specific characteristics that can dramatically impact investors. Great care and research should be taken before considering preferred shares in your portfolio.

Since they are thought of as a hybrid asset that has features that resemble both stocks and bonds, it makes sense to compare preferred shares to each of the traditional asset classes to assess whether they have a place in your portfolio.

Preferred shares vs. bonds

Both preferred shares and bonds are sought after by investors looking for income as both assets pay regular income and can be sensitive to changes in interest rates.

Pros of preferred shares over bonds

Higher yields

The first thing that many income-seeking investors tend to look at is yield. The higher the yield, the more income you receive relative to your initial investment.

For example, a bond might have a yield of 2%, meaning you would expect $2 in income for every $100 you invest. A preferred share might have a yield of 5%, which means you receive $5 in income for every $100 you invest.

Tax efficiency

Preferred shares are a form of equity—that means they pay dividends. Dividends receive a preferential tax treatment compared to interest income, which is what bonds pay.

In a 2015 paper, PWL Capital, a Canadian portfolio manager, looked at the tax savings of receiving $1,000 in income from preferred shares vs.

bonds.[38] An investor living in the high-tax province of Ontario in Canada (where I live), making $50,000 per year, would save $227 in taxes on $1,000 paid by preferred shares compared to $1,000 paid by bonds.

(This is a Canadian example of investments held in a taxable account. The numbers will be different in other countries.)

That is a significant amount of savings and a powerful advantage of preferred shares over bonds.

Cons of preferred shares over bonds

Complexity

If you think investing in bonds is complex, the world of preferred shares can feel overwhelming.

Most bonds share a common set of characteristics, which is not always the case with preferred shares. To illustrate this point, in the U.S. there are several different types of preferred shares:

- Callable shares: allow the issuing company to buy back the shares at a fixed price in the future.
- Convertible shares: can be converted into common shares at a fixed rate of preferred to common shares. For example, an investor may be able to convert one preferred share into two common shares of the issuing company.
- Cumulative preferred shares: require that any unpaid dividends be paid to preferred shareholders before common shareholders.

38 Bortolotti, D., Advisor, I., & Kerzérho, R. (2015). The Risks and Rewards of Canadian Preferred Shares. https://www.pwlcapital.com/wp-content/uploads/2018/06/2015-02-20_PWL_Kerzerho-Bortolotti_The-Role-of-Preferred-Shares-In-Your-Portfolio_Hyperlinked.pdf

- Participatory preference shares: pay additional dividends when the issuing company hits financial or earnings milestones.

Higher risk

With any income-oriented investment, the higher the yield, the more risk that is involved. Never lose sight of this: businesses don't make it a habit of simply giving you more income for free. Nor are markets so inefficient that a publicly-traded investment could offer a higher yield than bonds without taking on more risk. The rational investor never loses sight of the fact that risk and return are inseparable.

Preferred shares do not offer the same protections that bonds do. Unlike a bond, a company can miss a preferred share payment without going into default.

In the event of bankruptcy, bondholders will be repaid their initial capital before preferred shareholders.

There is always the risk that companies may—depending on the type of preferred share—redeem the shares if it is advantageous for them to do so.

In terms of volatility, preferred shares tend to be somewhere between corporate bonds and common stock.

Preferred shares vs. common stock

Preferred status

The name says it all: preferred shareholders receive preferential treatment when it comes to income. If a company has experienced a drop in revenue, it's the common shareholder dividend that will be cut before the preferred shareholder.

No voting rights

Preferred shareholders do not get to vote about how the company is run, which is a privilege enjoyed by common shareholders. If you are a rational investor who buys index funds, this is a non-factor as you wouldn't be eligible to vote on how individual companies are run.

Lower expected return

Preferred shares don't see price increases in the same way that common shares do, and as a result, preferred shares often have lower expected returns than common shares.

The two ingredients for a successful investment in preferred shares

Given their high yields, tax efficiency, and imperfect correlation with other asset classes, preferred shares are a compelling alternative investment in low interest rate environments.

Do you need them in your portfolio?

Probably not.

That being said, given their tax efficiency and imperfect correlation with common stock and bonds, a small allocation to preferred shares isn't likely to wreck your portfolio.

Just don't go overboard; there are two ingredients for the successful inclusion of preferred shares in your portfolio.

1. Moderation. Don't fall in love with the high yields; with that yield comes risk and only moderate upside potential.

2. Diversification. Given the risk and high levels of complexity, most investors would be best served not to buy individual preferred shares. Like with any investment, diversification helps reduce risk. If you are going to invest in preferred shares, consider investing in an ETF that holds a basket of preferred shares.

We should never underestimate the benefit of a simple portfolio consisting of a few globally diversified index funds. Adding preferred shares into the mix increases the complexity of your portfolio without increasing your expected returns.

Remember, the rational investor is focused on total returns, not yield.

Chapter 20: Hedge Funds: Higher Fees, Lower Returns

Warren Buffett knows how you should invest, and it's the opposite of what he does and what Wall Street does.

Buffett's famous hedge fund bet

In 2008, Buffett famously made a $1 million bet with a Wall Street hedge fund manager that a low-cost S&P 500 index fund would outperform a portfolio of hedge funds over 10 years.

Buffett's conviction was that the best way to invest for the vast majority of people is to invest in low-cost index funds. He didn't believe the high fees charged by Wall Street elites paid off for investors.

Buffett won the bet in a landslide.

This is despite the fact that the bet started on January 1st, 2008, mere months before the financial crisis would hit the market and essentially cut the S&P 500 in half. This is also when hedge funds are supposed to shine because they promise to "hedge" against this kind of market crash.

It's like the race began, and S&P 500 tripped over their shoelace at the starting line. But then got up and quickly sprinted past the hedge funds and easily left them in the dust.

This is because index funds are superior to hedge funds in almost every way.

The Intended purpose of hedge funds

The idea of hedge funds is to increase investor returns while reducing risk.

As the Buffett bet and the data we are about to review show, they generally do a poor job at increasing risk-adjusted returns.

Hedge funds come with massive fees. It's not uncommon for a hedge fund to charge investors a 2% annual fee for assets under management plus a 20% commission on excess performance.

Compare those fees to Vanguards S&P 500 index fund which, at the time I write this, charges investors an annual fee of 0.03% of assets under management.

But as active investors will tell you, the only thing that matters is your net-investment returns after fees.

This is where hedge funds are an utter failure.

The inefficiency of hedge funds

In a 2001 paper titled "Hedge Fund Performance: 1990-2000", researchers Harry Kat and Gaurav Amin examined the returns of 77 individual hedge funds and 13 hedge fund indices from 1990-2000 to investigate the claim by Wall Street that hedge funds offer investors superior risk-adjusted returns.[39]

They found 12/13 hedge fund indices and 72/77 individual hedge funds to be inefficient, providing a lower risk-adjusted return than the broad stock

39 Kat, H. M., & Amin, G. S. (2001, May 15). Hedge Fund Performance 1990-2000: Do the Money Machines Really Add Value? Papers.ssrn.com. https://papers.ssrn.com/sol3/papers.cfm?abstract_id=270074

market index. These inefficiencies amounted to 6.52% per year for individual hedge funds and 2.76% for hedge fund indices.

Two critical lessons we can learn from this research

First, diversification, no matter what asset class you invest in, works.

Much like picking stocks, picking individual hedge funds comes with idiosyncratic risk. This is the risk that is specific to an individual hedge fund but not the broader market of hedge funds. Think of idiosyncratic risk as the probability that you pick a below-average hedge fund manager.

Like with stocks, idiosyncratic risk can be diversified away. This is illustrated by the annual inefficiency dropping from 6.52% to 2.76% when investing in an index of hedge funds rather than an individual hedge fund.

Second, hedge funds are an inefficient investment.

No matter how you slice it, hedge funds have been getting their clock cleaned by low-cost index funds for decades.

Does the rational investor include hedge funds in their portfolio?

As a stand-alone investment, hedge funds are terrible. They provide higher fees and lower returns than index funds over the long run.

If the majority of your money were invested in hedge funds, you'd have less money than if you invested in index funds. This is especially true for the long-term investor. The longer the time horizon, the more likely index funds are to outperform.

If I were to play devil's advocate, I would point out one use for hedge funds which is a possible diversification benefit. Given that hedge funds have a lower correlation with the broader market, a small percentage of a portfolio dedicated to hedge funds might help lower the overall volatility of your portfolio, particularly in market downturns.

Having said that, here's why the rational investor avoids hedge funds.

Rational investors are, by definition, long-term investors. This means they are less concerned about short-term volatility and focused almost exclusively on maximizing wealth in the long term.

Maybe a hedge fund could help in the short term during a market crash, but over the next 50 years, the rational investor has every reason to expect that hedge fund to be a drag on returns.

Chapter 21: Private Equity: Good on paper, disappointing in reality

Private equity is an alternative asset class that does exactly what you'd think: invest in private businesses (companies that don't trade on the stock market).

On paper, it would appear that private equity deserves to be included in the portfolio of a rational investor. Historically private equity has provided higher returns than public companies with less day-to-day volatility.

However, when we look under the hood of private equity, we can see a big gap between the perception of this asset class and reality.

The theory of private equity returns

A 2020 paper titled "Demystifying Illiquid Assets: Expected Returns for Private Equity", published in the Journal of Alternative Investments, lays out four theoretical reasons that explain the returns of private equity.[40]

1. Equity risk. If you invest in a business, whether private or public, you are compensated for taking on risk. Private equity firms use more leverage (debt) than publically traded companies, potentially increasing risk and returns.
2. An illiquidity premium. Investors in private equity are often required to lock up their initial investment for 5-10 years. To compel

40 Demystifying Illiquid Assets: Expected Returns for Private Equity. (n.d.). Www.aqr.com. Retrieved May 30, 2022, from https://www.aqr.com/Insights/Research/White-Papers/Demystifying-Illiquid-Assets-Expected-Returns-for-Private-Equity#:~:text=The%20growing%20interest%20in%20private

investors to lock their money away, they must be compensated with higher returns which is referred to as the illiquidity premium.

3. Size. Private equity firms tend to buy smaller companies, which gives them exposure to the size factor which is based on historical evidence that smaller companies outperform large companies.
4. Value. Private equity firms buy companies with low valuation multiples, which gives them exposure to the value premium which is based on historical evidence that companies with low valuations outperform.

Compared to what?

From 1986-2017 private equity firms outperformed the S&P 500 by 2.3% per year.

However, the paper in the Journal of Alternative Investments makes an important point. Comparing private equity returns to a benchmark like the S&P 500—which consists of large companies— is not appropriate. Given the previously discussed factors that explain private equity returns, it's more appropriate to compare performance with an index on leveraged small cap value stocks because they share a similar risk profile.

Another paper, written by Harvard professor Erik Stafford, also concluded that private equity returns could be replicated with a leveraged portfolio of small-cap value stocks.[41]

From 1986 to 2017, private equity firms underperformed publicly traded small-cap value stocks by 1.6% per year.

---

41 Replicating Private Equity with Value Investing, Homemade Leverage, and Hold-to-Maturity Accounting - Working Paper - Faculty & Research - Harvard Business School. (n.d.). Www.hbs.edu. Retrieved May 30, 2022, from https://www.hbs.edu/faculty/Pages/item.aspx?num=50433

Private equity is risker than it looks

Private equity firms do not use the same method of accounting as publicly traded companies. As the paper from the Journal of Alternative Investments points out, this leads to the volatility of private equity being underreported.

Private equity has created an illusion of low volatility, which is attractive to investors—often causing them to overpay for private equity. When you invest in public companies or buy an index fund, you can track the volatility in real-time on your phone.

Some investors would rather overpay for private equity than simply stop looking at their phones.

Does the rational investor include private equity in their portfolio?

The rational investor should add private equity to their portfolio of stock and bond index funds if private equity offers returns that can't be replicated through publically traded companies.

Here's what the evidence suggests:

- Private equity returns can be replicated through a portfolio of publically traded small-cap value companies.
- The fees for private equity are higher than index funds.
- Private equity is much less liquid and provides weak compensation for that lack of liquidity.
- The smoothing of private equity returns can make private equity appear less risky than it really is.

There's no rational case to include private equity in a portfolio given the evidence.

Chapter 22:
Gold: Safe Haven or Shiny Distraction?

Gold is one of the most popular alternative investments to traditional portfolios of stocks and bonds.

There are two primary reasons investors buy gold.

1. It's thought of as a hedge against inflation.
2. It's seen as a "safe haven asset".

In this chapter, we review the evidence of each of these claims and come to a clear decision about whether or not the rational investor includes gold in their portfolio.

The Golden Dilemma

The definitive research paper on gold is "The Golden Dilemma", written by Campbell Harvey and Claude Erb[1]. In this paper, Harvey and Erb examine the value of gold over a 2,000+ year timeframe. It's an incredibly detailed paper with some valuable findings of including gold in a portfolio.[42]

Gold as an inflation hedge

Harvey and Erb found that gold tends to keep up with inflation and "hold its value over long periods of time".

But just because gold holds its value over the long run does not make it an effective hedge against inflation. To understand why that is, you need to

42 Erb, C., & Harvey, C. (2013). NBER WORKING PAPER SERIES THE GOLDEN DILEMMA. https://www.nber.org/system/files/working_papers/w18706/w18706.pdf

understand that for an asset to be a *hedge* against inflation; it must increase in value at the same time inflation rises, so as to offset the impact of unexpectedly high inflation.

If gold is an inflation hedge and inflation is 6%, gold should rise by 6%. This is not how it plays out in real life because the price of gold is constantly moving up and down.

Harvey and Erb document gold's ineffectiveness as a hedge against inflation from 1975–2011. To quote their findings:

> *"The price of gold swings widely around the CPI. The inflation derived price of gold and the actual price of gold have rarely been equal."*

Gold is an effective inflation hedge if you plan on living for centuries

A fascinating aspect of The Golden Dilemma paper is that Harvey and Erb examine the value of gold dating back to when Caesar Augustus ruled the Roman empire from 27 B.C. to 14 A.D.

The Romans kept meticulous records by ancient standards, so historians know exactly how much the Romans paid various ranking soldiers and military officers.

Roman legionaries (equivalent rank of a "private" in the U.S. military) were paid 2.31 ounces of gold a year, while a centurion (similar rank to a "captain") was paid 38.58 ounces per year.

They found that when measured in U.S. dollars, Roman soldiers and modern soldiers in the U.S. army were paid roughly the same amount.

This confirms two things:

1. When measured in centuries, gold has kept up with inflation.
2. Its long-run, expected "Real" returns are close to zero.

Gold is not an effective hedge against inflation due to its short-term volatility, but if you plan on living for the next 2,000 years, it might be an effective way to maintain your purchasing power.

To quote Harvey and Erb:

> *"In normal times, gold does not seem to be a good hedge of realized or unexpected short-run inflation. Gold may very well be a long-run inflation hedge. However, the long-run may be longer than an investor's investment time horizon or life span."*

Gold as a safe haven asset

The diehard gold investors view the asset as a "safe haven" investment; they believe gold will increase in value when traditional assets like stocks are crashing. The general idea is that when there is fear of a deep economic recession, people will flock to "safe" assets like gold.

Some of the most high-profile and diehard gold investors believe that gold will revert back to the primary means of exchange if the world economy comes crashing down. Let's dispense with this line of thinking. The rational investor will always bet on the world *not ending*.

- If you bet on the world not ending and you are right, you win.
- If you bet on the world not ending and you are wrong, what's happening with your portfolio should be of little concern.

Do you really think you'll be dragging your gold bars around and exchanging them for food and shelter in a post-apocalyptic world? If so, you are reading the wrong book.

Even if you don't expect to be shaving off a gold bar to buy eggs and milk, the question remains is gold a safe haven asset? Harvey and Erb provided two characteristics of what a safe haven asset might look like:

1. It should have a stable value during a "time of stress".
2. It should be accessible to investors during that time of stress.

By those two characteristics, for gold to be a safe haven asset, it would need to hold its value, and investors should be able to get a hold of their gold and convert it into cash when they need it.

Harvey and Erb found that between 1975 and 2012 gold had negative returns in 17% of the months that the S&P 500 had a negative return. Meaning, for every five months, the stock market goes down, the price of gold also goes down. That implies a low correlation with stocks but not exactly a reliable "safe haven".

On the issue of accessibility, Harvey and Erb point to anecdotal evidence to suggest physical gold is difficult to access during times of stress. Sometime around 400 AD, when the Roman Empire was falling apart, a wealthy family buried their gold, and that gold remained buried until researchers unearthed it in 1992—nearly 1,600 years later. The fact of that matter is that gold is a heavy, physical asset giving it a low market value to pound ratio.

Gold does a poor job of satisfying either of Harvey and Erb's characteristics of what a safe haven asset looks like.

Gold has no productive value

Warren Buffett made his thoughts on gold as an investible asset crystal clear in his 2011 letter to shareholders of Berkshire Hathaway.[43]

Buffett pointed out that gold has no productive value beyond its use in some industrial capacities.

To illustrate the non-productive nature of gold, Buffett made a comparison that at the time he wrote the letter in 2011, all the gold in the world—which at the time was worth $9.6 trillion—would buy:

- 400 million acres of farmland in the U.S. with an output of about $200 billion annually,
- 16 Exxon Mobils with combined earnings of $640 billion,
- while leaving $1 trillion in cash left over.

Buffett asked what investor in their right mind would choose to own gold over those productive assets? Here's his full quote:

> *"A century from now, the 400 million acres of farmland will have produced staggering amounts of corn, wheat, cotton, and other crops – and will continue to produce that valuable bounty, whatever the currency may be.*
>
> *Exxon Mobil will probably have delivered trillions of dollars in dividends to its owners and will also hold assets worth many more trillions (and, remember, you get 16 Exxons).*

43 (2011). Letter To the Shareholders of Berkshire Hathaway Inc [Review of Letter To the Shareholders of Berkshire Hathaway Inc]. Berkshire Hathaway Inc. https://www.berkshirehathaway.com/letters/2011ltr.pdf

The 170,000 tons of gold will be unchanged in size and still incapable of producing anything.

You can fondle the cube, but it will not respond."

Does the rational investor include gold in their portfolio?

Given gold's popular narratives driven by enthusiastic supporters and its low correlation to the stock market, it's easy to understand why many investors are happy to include gold in their portfolios.

However, the rational investor looks beyond narratives and examines the evidence. The best evidence available to us at the time I write this suggests that gold is neither an effective inflation hedge nor a safe haven asset. The real expected return of gold over the long run is roughly zero. This is because, as Warren Buffett points out—gold is a non-productive asset.

For all of these reasons, the rational investor does not include gold in their portfolio.

Chapter 23: Can Crypto Help Diversify a Portfolio?

The perfect investment portfolio has to meet two criteria.

1. Provides high enough expected returns to meet your financial goals.
2. Minimizes volatility to the point where you can stay invested.

Risk and reward are paired at the hip

Want higher returns?

You have to take on more risk.

But if you take on more risk than you can handle, you won't be able to stay invested long enough to build wealth and hit your goals.

Diversification helps investors thread the risk-reward needle

The basic premise of a diversified portfolio is to help investors hit that sweet spot where they are taking on enough risk to capture the returns they need while not being so volatile that they are unable or unwilling to stay invested.

For diversification to work, the assets in a portfolio should have a low correlation—meaning they don't always move in the same direction—and critically, they should maintain a low correlation during downturns.

This is the rationale behind the classic 60/40 portfolio, which is made up of 60% stocks and 40% bonds.

- Stocks provide higher returns, but it's a bumpy ride.
- Bonds have lower expected returns but are less volatile.

Adding bonds to a portfolio has historically provided exceptional diversification benefits because bonds tend to maintain their value or increase in value when stocks are falling—helping to smooth out the ride enough for investors to say in their seats.

Vanguard has compiled some interesting data on returns and volatility of portfolios that range from 100% bonds to 100% equities. The following data is from 1926-2020.[44]

100% bonds

- Average annual return: 6.1%
- This portfolio had a negative return in 1 of every 5 years.
- Worst year: 1969 with an 8.1% loss.

20% stocks-80% bonds

- Average annual return: 7.2%
- This portfolio had a negative return in 1 of every 6 years.
- Worst year: 1931 with a 10.1% loss.

40% stocks-60% bonds

- Average annual return: 8.2%
- This portfolio had a negative return in 1 of every 5 years.
- Worst year: 1931 with an 18.4% loss.

60% stocks-40% bonds

- Average annual return: 8.6%
- This portfolio had a negative return in 1 of every 4.3 years.
- Worst year: 1931 with a 26.6% loss.

44 Model Portfolio Allocation | Vanguard. (n.d.). Investor.vanguard.com. https://investor.vanguard.com/investor-resources-education/education/model-portfolio-allocation

80% stocks-20% bonds

- Average annual return: 9.8%
- This portfolio had a negative return in 1 of every 4 years.
- Worst year: 1931 with a 34.9% loss

100% stocks

- Average annual return: 10.3%
- This portfolio had a negative return in 1 of every 3.8 years.
- Worst year: 1931 with a 43.1% loss.

This paints a perfect picture of what diversification is supposed to do: trading in returns for lower volatility. Remember, risk and returns are paired at the hip. Many investors focus on the returns and minimize what it feels like to experience the spectacular lows that risky assets like stocks go through.

In 1931 the U.S. stock market lost 43.1% of its value which was the worst year in the record books. This also happened to be during the great depression. As the data shows, the more weighted towards bonds a portfolio was, the less painful 1931 was for investors.

- 100% stocks—43.1% loss
- 80% stocks/20% bonds—34.9% loss
- 60% stocks/40% bonds—26.6% loss
- 40% stocks/60% bonds—18.4% loss
- 20% stocks/80% bonds—10.1% loss.

This is why the "60/40" portfolio of stocks and bonds has long been the poster child of diversification. Many investors have seen that as the sweet spot between high returns and a level of volatility they can stomach.

What does the data say about crypto as a diversifying asset?

As I write this in April 2022, we have very little data to make definitive conclusions. Bitcoin was only created in 2009, and the crypto market has only begun to expand in the last several years. It's a very new asset class, and as the years roll on, the data may begin to tell a different story. But here's what it tells us today.

On the positive side, crypto assets have a surprisingly low correlation with stocks and bonds. Research from Morningstar shows that the correlation between the 10 largest digital assets and stocks was only 0.32 from 2018-2021.[45]

But for an asset to provide meaningful diversification benefits to a portfolio primarily weighted in stocks, the diversifying asset should maintain a low correlation when stocks are falling. This is where crypto fails as a diversifying asset. The correlation between crypto-assets and U.S. stocks spiked to 0.75 during the 2020 COVID market crash.

To make matters worse, the more established crypto assets like Bitcoin and Ether have seen their correlation with stocks increase as time goes on. Once a crypto asset gains widespread adoption from institutional investors, it becomes increasingly correlated with other risky assets like stocks, which dramatically reduces any diversification benefits.

Crypto is too volatile to be an effective diversifying asset

Morningstar's report titled "mind the gap" provides valuable insight into the damage investors do to themselves by fiddling with their portfolios.[46]

45 Is Cryptocurrency Really a Portfolio Diversifier? (2022, April 18). Morningstar, Inc. https://www.morningstar.com/articles/1088689/is-cryptocurrency-really-a-portfolio-diversifier

46 Mind the Gap | Morningstar. (n.d.). Www.morningstar.com. https://www.morningstar.com/lp/mind-the-gap

Morningstar looked at the average return of investment funds over the past 10 years and compared that to the actual return that investors in those funds received.

- Stock investors underperformed their investments by 0.56% per year.
- Bond investors underperformed their investments by 0.55% per year.
- Investors in alternative assets underperformed by 1.44% per year.

If an investor put their money into a fund that bought "alternative" assets (like crypto) and that fund returned 2.44%, the investor would only have realized a return of 1% on average.

Why?

Because rather than buying and holding investments, most people try (and fail) to time the market.

What little data we have on crypto at this point paints a clear picture: crypto investors pile on when things are going great and rush to the door at the first sign of volatility.

- From January 2020 to November 2021, the global market cap for crypto assets increased by 1,400%.
- During this time, a record amount of new money was being invested in crypto.
- Over a 3-month period from November 2021 to January 2022, crypto assets lost roughly half (47%) of their value.
- The crypto crash corresponds with negative fund flows into crypto assets.

Investors bought the crypto hype at its peak and then sold after prices crashed. That's what it means to buy high and sell low, which is the easiest way to lose money.

Does the rational investor include crypto in their portfolio?

The rational buy-and-hold investor who buys a handful of globally diversified index funds will pass on investing in crypto as a way to further diversify their portfolio.

While the average correlation between stocks and crypto appears low, those correlations spike during downturns in the stock market. A good diversifying asset is supposed to help cushion the fall in stocks. Crypto not only falls with stocks, but it falls even harder.

The rational investor makes evidence-based decisions, and the current evidence we have is that bonds still make more sense as a diversifying asset to stocks than crypto or other alternative investments.

Chapter 24: Why You're Bad at Trading Stocks

In Chapter 11, we reviewed the terrible odds of picking individual stocks.

At first glance, a chapter on "trading" stocks might feel redundant. But, picking individual stocks and holding them for an extended period of time is a completely different animal than day trading. There are a lot of charlatans who will try their hardest to get you to buy their $3,000 online course that promises to "teach you how to day trade for a living."

If you ever feel even the slightest inclination to fork over your hard-earned cash for one of these courses, reread this chapter and the evidence I am about to lay out.

What is day trading?

As the name implies, day trading is when assets are bought and sold over a very short period of time—often within the same trading day.

Two common financial assets that day traders buy and sell are:

1. Stocks
2. Options

The reality of trading stocks

The top 0.5% of stocks bought every day on Robinhood lose about 4.7% over the next month.

That was one of the findings from a recent research paper titled "Attention Induced Trading and Returns: Evidence from Robinhood Users."[47] The researchers studied data from Robinhood to determine the impact on individuals' trading and stock prices.

They found the most intensely bought stocks on the app tend to lose money after users jump on the bandwagon. Not a surprising outcome, as this is the exact phenomenon we reviewed in Chapter 15 during our discussion of thematic ETFs. But it's interesting to have empirical evidence backing up what should be obvious: trading stocks is an easy way to lose money.

The researchers hypothesize two reasons Robinhood users underperform:

1. Robinhood attracts inexperienced investors.
2. Unique features of the app help facilitate "attention-induced trading".

Let's review the evidence that explains why those two ingredients are a recipe for terrible investment returns.

Here's why you're bad at trading stocks

A 1998 paper written by Terrance Odean, a professor at the Haas School of Business, University of California Berkeley, asked a simple question: *"Do Investors Trade Too Much?"*[48]

(Spoiler: yes, they do)

47 Barber, B. M., Huang, X., Odean, T., & Schwarz, C. (2020). Attention Induced Trading and Returns: Evidence from Robinhood Users. SSRN Electronic Journal. https://doi.org/10.2139/ssrn.3715077

48 Odean, T. (1998). Do Investors Trade Too Much? SSRN Electronic Journal. https://doi.org/10.2139/ssrn.94143

Odean analyzed 10,000 trading accounts at discount brokerages to understand the performance of retail investors who regularly trade stocks. He found that retail investors were engaging in excessive trading that caused them to underperform.

To make money trading stocks requires you to get two things right.

1. Buying the right stock at the right price.
2. Selling that stock at a higher price and trading it for a better-performing stock.

Odean found that the average retail investor was not that bad at buying the right stocks; the problem was they were terrible at knowing when to sell those stocks.

They couldn't stick the landing.

Here's how Odean phrased it.

> *"On average, the stocks that traders sell outperform the stocks they buy next."*

Translation*: traders would make more money by simply holding the stocks they have rather than continuing to trade—the term for this would be excessive trading.*

Why selling stocks is so difficult

To understand why it's so hard to nail the sell-side of a stock trade, professor Odean gives us a lesson in behavioral finance.

Professor Odean explains the concept of a "reference price", which is what an investor "*perceives*" to be their breakeven point where they would be indifferent on whether to hold or sell a stock. The word "perceives" is the keyword there because the wild swings in stock prices can radically alter our perceived breakeven point.

In the paper, Professor Odean uses the example of a homeowner who bought their house for $100,000—if that seems like an absurdly low price for a house remember, this is a 1998 paper.

- $100,000 is their breakeven point.
- But if the housing market goes bonkers and the price increases to $200,000, after a while, the homeowner adopts $200,000 as their new breakeven point.
- They might be unwilling to sell for less than $200,000 even if the market dictates a lower price in the future.

Think about how that might play out in the situation with a stock.

- You buy a stock at $30 per share.
- It quickly jumps to $60.
- Eventually, you might view $60 as your new reference price. If you sell below this, you "feel" like you are losing money even though you're not.
- So you hang onto the stock even as it continues to slide downwards.

The opposite is also true.

- You buy a stock for $60 per share.
- It quickly drops to $30. This really hurts as investors feel much more intense emotions from losing money than they do from making money.
- After a while, the price rises to $40.

- You'd be more willing to sell that stock at $40 even though you're losing money because your reference price has dropped below your actual breakeven point of $60.
- You're desperate to get out of this "loser" and are willing to sell at a loss.
- Then you buy a new stock and repeat the process even as the stock you just sold climbs back up to $60 and beyond.

Trading "popular stocks" is an easy way to lose money

There are tens of thousands of publically traded companies in the world, but most day traders focus on a tiny fraction of those stocks.

We even have a name for them now, "Meme-stocks". These are stocks that are generating lots of buzz online. Limiting your investment opportunities to the select number of stocks that are driving the news is an easy way to lose money.

A 2021 research paper titled "Internet Search, Fund Flows, and Fund Performance", used Google search volume as a measure of investor attention to explore the connection between investment funds that were grabbing headlines and the future performance of those investments.[49]

If an investment fund saw a spike in Google searches, the researchers wanted to know how much money poured into the funds after that spike in traffic and how the fund performed.

49 Chen, H.-Y., Chen, H.-C., & Lai, C. W. (2021). Internet search, fund flows, and fund performance. Journal of Banking & Finance, 129, 106166. https://doi.org/10.1016/j.jbankfin.2021.106166

They found that retail investors were more likely to buy these funds that were generating online buzz. Unsurprisingly, these attention-driven investors had negative future returns.

It's a pretty simple picture to paint.

- Search traffic for an investment fund is highly correlated with its past returns.
- Once a fund does really well, it gets investors' attention.
- Investors pile into the fund, expecting the fund to continue to outperform.
- This is called "return chasing".
- Predictably, these superstar funds tend to perform poorly after everyone has piled into them.
- **The most recent investors who bought at the top lose the most money.**

The most relevant quote from the paper:

> "*Investors cannot generate superior fund-related future returns when they exclusively follow online buzz and associated suggestions.*"

This explains why the most traded stocks on Robinhood lost 4.7% the following month. Making investment decisions based on what's "popular" is completely devoid of logic.

To make matters worse, social media influencers often encourage inexperienced users to engage in higher-risk, complex trading schemes like options trading, where losses can mount even quicker. Oftentimes, these same influencers are selling a product, "teaching" you how to make money by investing as they do.

Trading options

Call and put options are a contract that gives the option holder the right but not the obligation to buy or sell a specific asset at a specified price (referred to as the strike price) within a specific time range.

Call options provide the holder the right, but not the obligation, to buy a stock at a specified price within a predetermined time range.

If the stock price does not reach the specified price, the option expires, and the option becomes worthless. To obtain this right, you would have to pay an "option premium". If you do not exercise your call option, your loss is equal to the amount of the option premium.

Put Options provide the holder the right, but not the obligation, to sell a stock at a specified price within a predetermined time range. Put simply (I could not resist the pun), a put option is the opposite of a call option.

In recent years, discount brokerages and online trading platforms have encouraged individual investors to engage in options trading. They marketed this as a way of "democratizing" finance.

To be clear, the world of investing was democratized decades ago by Jack Bogle and Vanguard when they made it easy and cheap for retail investors to buy the entire stock market through low-cost index funds. The investment revolution is over; we won.

The problem for Wall Street is that given the low costs of index funds, the only way to make real money providing them is to have north of a trillion dollars in assets under management—a feat that only a handful of firms ever achieve. Instead, they introduce complex products that investors don't need and brand it as democratizing the investment for "the little guy or gal".

Here's a rule of thumb: If Wall Street or, even worse, Silicon Valley tells you they are "democratizing" an asset class, hold onto your wallet and run the opposite direction.

Examining the evidence of how retail investors do with options trading

In a 2021 paper titled "Trading Behavior of Retail Investors in Derivatives Markets: Evidence from Mini Options", Li et al. used so-called "mini options" to compare how retail investors stack up against professional traders in the options market.[50]

They found that retail options traders had a much more limited attention span than institutional traders. Retail investors focused the majority of their trades when the stock market opened. That timing may also line up with retail investors having to report to their day jobs. This intense trading at the opening bell leads to poor performance compared to the institutional traders.

Imagine trying to outperform professional investors when the bulk of your trades need to be done during your 15-minute coffee break.

Retail traders were also more likely to trade intensely after headline-grabbing events and reduce trading volumes on quiet news days. Given the reasonable efficiency of the stock market, big headline news gets priced into stocks within seconds.

By the time a retail investor reads the headline and logs into their trading account, the news is already baked into the price. Further trading in an attempt to exploit that news is a pointless waste of time and money.

---

50 Li, Y., Zhao, C., & Zhong, Z. (2021). Trading behavior of retail investors in derivatives markets: Evidence from Mini options. Journal of Banking & Finance, 133, 106250. https://doi.org/10.1016/j.jbankfin.2021.106250

Day trading is a terrible way to try and earn a living

Let's circle back to those online influencers who want to sell you a course about how you can make a living day trading. Let's look at what the evidence has to say about the prospects of anyone trying to make a living as a trader.

A 2019 paper titled "Day Trading for a Living?" written by Chague et al. studied how much money day traders in Brazil made between 2013-2015.[51]The following quote from the paper that will tell you all you need to know about the prospects of a career in day trading.

> *"97% of all individuals who persisted for more than 300 days lost money. Only 1.1% earned more than the Brazilian minimum wage and only 0.5% earned more than the initial salary of a bank teller—all with great risk."*

So, if you want to combine the hourly wage of someone flipping burgers with the risk of an entrepreneur then day trading is the career for you!

Chague et al. also found "no evidence of learning", among day traders. Keep that in mind the next time someone asks you to pay thousands of dollars to learn how to trade for a living.

3 questions day traders should ask themselves

Question 1: Who is on the other side of this trade?

Every time you buy a stock, there is someone else on the other end of that trade who is willing to sell that stock to you at the price you asked for.

---

51 Chague, F., De-Losso, R., & Giovannetti, B. (2019). Day Trading for a Living? SSRN Electronic Journal. https://doi.org/10.2139/ssrn.3423101

Ask yourself, who is that person? Odds are that it is a financial professional with a great deal of experience or knowledge of the company being traded.

Question 2: Why is that other person selling this stock?

The person on the other end of the trade currently owns that stock and is willing to sell it to you.

Ask yourself why they are willing to sell?

The most likely reason is that they feel the stock is overvalued at its current price or has low expected returns in the future.

Question 3: What do I know that the other person does not?

Once you have asked yourself who you are trading with and why they are willing to sell, the final question you need to ask is, what do you know that the other person does not?

What information do you have about the company you are investing in that makes you confident that buying it at its current price is a good investment. Keep in mind that the person on the other end of the trade thinks it's a good idea to sell this stock at its current price.

Anyone who honestly sought the answer to these questions would not day trade.

Does the rational investor day trade?

No.

Chapter 25: Factor Investing: The Only Rational Way to "Beat the Market"

Throughout this book, I have, on occasion, made references to "small-cap" and "value" stocks. You have likely heard these terms before if you follow the financial media, but these are far more than just investing buzzwords. These so-called risk "factors" have as much academic evidence supporting them as index investing.

A word of caution

This chapter is by far the "nerdiest" chapter in the book. The theory and empirical evidence supporting factor investing are compelling. But understanding the theory of factor investing is one thing—implementing it in a portfolio in an efficient manner is another.

If you value simplicity, skip this chapter and stick with a simple portfolio of globally diversified, market-cap weighted index funds. Index funds will serve the long-term investor well, and most people reading this would be better off sticking with the simple indexing strategy.

A portfolio of market-cap weighted index funds is like a sundae. Nobody in history has ever been unhappy after being handed a bowl of ice cream and chocolate.

Factor investing is like the cherry on top of the sundae. Maybe you like cherries, or maybe you view them as unnecessary. The point is that you need the sundae; it's non-negotiable. Whether or not you want the cherry on top comes down to personal taste.

If you value optimizing long-run expected returns over a simplicity or you simply want to learn more about how different stocks are priced, continue reading for an overview of factor investing.

Back to basics

Investors earn returns in exchange for taking on risks. Factor investing aims to maximize returns by targeting different risks within a portfolio.

Let's start the discussion by reviewing the primary investment factor, the systematic risk of the entire stock market. When you invest in the stock market through a market-cap weighted index fund, you are taking on the systematic risk of the whole stock market.

That is why the stock market has higher expected returns than the so-called "risk-free" assets like short-term government bonds. **The difference between the investment returns provided by the stock market and a risk-free asset is referred to as the risk premium.**

The risk premium is positive in years where stocks outperform risk-free assets and negative in years where stocks underperform risk-free assets.

The risk premium is not guaranteed to be positive and can be negative over long stretches. Think of the so-called "lost decade", which was bookended by the dot com crash and the great financial crisis of 2008-2009. From 2000-2010 the S&P 500 provided annualized returns of negative 0.95%.

However, over the long run, the risk premium has been positive. At the beginning of this book, we reviewed the evidence that no investor has ever lost money when investing in an S&P 500 index fund and sitting on it for 20+ years.

Factor premiums

As we just discussed, the first and most important factor is the systematic risk of the entire stock market. The difference in returns between the stock market and risk-free assets is the risk premium, your reward for taking on market risk.

Factor investing is about targeting unique risks that are independent of the total stock market. Investors are compensated for taking on these additional risks through higher expected returns. **We refer to these higher expected returns achieved through exposure to unique risk factors as factor premiums.**

Factor premiums are positive in years that the unique risk factor provides greater returns than the market and negative in years they do not.

Much like the risk premium, factor premiums can be negative for long stretches of time. However, in the long run, we expect that factor premiums to be positive.

Before we jump into the research that supports positive factor premiums, let's take a moment to clarify what factors I am referring to.

What are these unique risk factors?

There are many different factors that investment companies will trot out to promote their fund. The rational investor looks at the best available evidence, and when it comes to factor investing, the best available evidence begins with a 2015 paper titled "A Five-Factor Asset Pricing Model" written by Eugene Fama and Ken French.[52]

52 Fama, E. F., & French, K. R. (2015). A five-factor asset pricing model. Journal of Financial Economics, 116(1), 1–22. https://doi.org/10.1016/j.jfineco.2014.10.010

In the paper, Fama, and French identify five unique risk factors for equity investors.

1. The systematic risk of the total stock market.
2. Value
3. Size
4. Profitability
5. Investment patterns

We have already discussed the evidence for the first factor (market risk), so let's discuss the other four risk factors.

The value premium

What if I told you there was an investment strategy that was the opposite of meme-stock investing? Is that something you might be interested in?

It's called value investing.

A value stock is a company whose stock price trades at a low price relative to its underlying fundamentals.

There are not many "famous examples" of value stocks to point to, which tells you a lot about value investing. Value investors do not invest in sexy name brand companies with eccentric founders who sell the investors on a grand vision of the future.

The best way to understand value investing is to start by thinking about Tesla in 2021 and then imagining what a company would look like if it were the exact opposite of Tesla.

Think railroads, oil companies, and banks.

What is the value premium?

In their 2020 paper titled "The Value Premium", Eugene Fama and Ken French define the value premium as the return of value stocks minus the return of the general stock market.[53]

If value stocks outperform the general stock market, the value premium will be positive.

Why does the value premium exist?

There are two competing theories.

1. **Investors misprice value stocks.**
2. **Value stocks are risker than growth stocks.** If investors are to take on additional risk, they need to be compensated by buying a company at a lower price.

Fama and French reject the mispricing theory arguing that if value stocks were not, in fact, riskier than growth stocks, the value factor would disappear due to opportunistic traders arbitrating the value premium away.

The risk explanation for value stocks is in line with the efficient market theory. In this view, value stocks are priced efficiently and reflect the inherent riskiness of the company.

Is the value premium dead?

The 2010s and early 2020s were not kind to value investors, with mega-cap growth stocks like Tesla outperforming value stocks by a wide margin.

53 Fama, E. F., & French, K. R. (2020). The Value Premium. SSRN Electronic Journal. https://doi.org/10.2139/ssrn.3525096

That has led to many investors and pundits asking if the value premium is dead?

In their 2020 paper on the value premium, Fama and French answer that question by, you guessed it, examining the evidence.

First, they found that from 1963 to 2019, the value premium was positive, meaning value stocks outperformed the general stock market. However, value stocks performed much better in the early sample (1963-1991) than in the later sample (1991-2019).

Value vs. growth over the long-run

To dig deeper into this question, Fama and French constructed seven different portfolios.

1. Growth stocks
2. Large-cap growth stocks
3. Small-cap growth stocks
4. Value stocks
5. Large-cap value stocks
6. Small-cap value stocks
7. The total stock market

Then they examined how each of these portfolios of value and growth stocks performed relative to the total market in the 56 years from 1963 to 2019.

From 1963-2019 none of the growth stock portfolios outperformed the total stock market.

The value premium ebbs and flows

From 1963-1991 all three value portfolios provided exceptional outperformance.

- Large-cap value stocks outperformed the market by 0.36% per month.
- Small-cap value stocks outperformed the market by 0.58% per month.
- All value stocks outperformed the market by 0.42% per month.

But from 1991-2019, the value premium weakened across the board.

- Large-cap value stocks outperformed the market by 0.05% per month.
- Small-cap value stocks outperformed the market by 0.33% per month.
- All value stocks outperformed the market by 0.11% per month.

Fama and French conclude that there is no statistical evidence that the value premium disappears entirely in the second half of the sample. This means the rational way to look at the value premium is using the whole data set from 1963-1991.

- Large-cap value stocks outperformed the market by 0.21% per month.
- Small-cap value stocks outperformed the market by 0.45% per month.
- All value stocks outperformed the market by 0.26% per month.

The value premium is not dead, but it can slip into a coma

So what is a value investor to make of this evidence?

First, value investing only makes sense if you have a long investment horizon: think decades, not years. Over the 56 years in the Fama-French data, value stocks outperformed, particularly small-cap value stocks.

Second, the cost of that outperformance is higher volatility in your portfolio.

Third, value investors must be prepared to underperform for very long periods. Due to the volatility of the value premium, there will be years or even decades when value stocks underperform growth stocks and the broader market.

Value investing is a viable long-term strategy for a buy-and-hold investor. But if you get nervous about the volatility of investing in a simple index fund, value investing may not be for you. If you can't hold on for decades, you're unlikely to capture the value premium.

What is the size premium?

The size premium was first discovered in a 1981 paper titled "The Relationship Between Return and Market Value of Common Stocks", written by Rolf Banz.[54] Banz found that small companies consistently have higher risk-adjusted returns than large companies.

The size premium is the difference in returns between small and large firms. When the size premium is positive, small stocks outperform large

54 Banz, R. W. (1981). The relationship between return and market value of common stocks. Journal of Financial Economics, 9(1), 3–18. https://doi.org/10.1016/0304-405x(81)90018-0

stocks, and that is why the shorthand for the size premium is Small Minus Big (SMB).

Why does the size premium exist?

Smaller companies are often considered to be inherently riskier than larger companies. To incentivize investors to take on that risk, they need to be compensated with higher expected returns.

In a 2018 paper titled "The Size Effect Continues to be Relevant When Estimating the Cost of Capital", author Roger Grabowski provides several risk-based explanations for why smaller companies are risker than big companies.[55]

- Larger companies can easily enter the market of the small company and take market share.
- Large companies have more resources to weather economic recessions.
- Small companies have less money to invest in R&D and advertising than large companies.
- The market for smaller companies is less liquid than for large companies.
- It's more difficult for small companies to raise capital.
- Smaller companies tend to have a less diverse customer base compared to larger companies.

For all of these reasons, small stocks are considered riskier, which means investors expect to be compensated with higher expected returns.

55 Grabowski, R. J. (2018, October 30). The Size Effect Continues to be Relevant When Estimating the Cost of Capital. Papers.ssrn.com. https://papers.ssrn.com/sol3/papers.cfm?abstract_id=3275366

Is the size premium dead?

Ask anyone who knows, and they'll tell you that "size matters, if you control your junk." Get your mind out of the gutter. That is the title of a 2018 paper published in the Journal of Financial Economics which provided breakthrough insight into the size premium.[56]

The size premium has long been thought of as playing second fiddle to the value premium. The size premium has a spotty and inconsistent track record and has been found to be extremely weak in international stocks. This has prompted many investors and researchers to ask if the size premium remains relevant.

Controlling for junk revives the size premium

The researchers behind the 2018 paper found that the magnitude and consistency of the size premium is revived by removing the low quality or "junky" companies from the small-cap universe.

The researchers used various definitions of "quality" and junk, and all found that removing junk—no matter how you define it— from the small-cap stocks greatly enhances the size premium.

One of the ways they controlled for quality was using the Asness et al. (2014) quality minus junk (QMJ) factor, which is long quality stocks and short junk stocks.[57]

---

56 Asness, C. S., Frazzini, A., Israel, R., Moskowitz, T. J., & Pedersen, L. H. (2018). Size matters, if you control your junk. SSRN Electronic Journal. https://doi.org/10.2139/ssrn.2553889

57 Asness, C. S., Frazzini, A., & Pedersen, L. H. (2013). Quality minus junk. SSRN Electronic Journal. https://doi.org/10.2139/ssrn.2312432

Controlling for quality increased the size premium from 14 basis points to 49 basis points per month.

To quote the paper:

> *"Overall, the results indicate that all of the measures of quality are negatively related to size and are helpful in resurrecting the size premium, even over different sample periods, with the results not particularly sensitive to any particular measure of quality."*

Translation: The size premium delivers tremendous returns when you remove the least profitable small-cap stocks.

So-called "small-cap growth stocks" with weak profitability or "junky" companies have been such terrible investments that they drag down all small stocks when they are left in the sample.

Removing junk increases the consistency of the size premium

The 20-year period from 1980-1999 was a very bad time for small-cap stocks. During that time, the size premium was negative 11 basis points per month.

Think of a 25-year-old investor in 1980 who started investing in small-cap stocks. That investor would underperform the market until they were 45-years old. Of course, the investor would have almost certainly tapped out and switched strategies long before that.

It's nice to read in academic journals that small-cap stocks tend to outperform. But it takes a level of faith that is hard to imagine to continue sticking to that strategy when you're getting punched in the mouth for 20 years straight.

However, when controlling for quality (removing the junk), the size premium explodes during that 1980-1999 period, increasing from negative 11 basis points to 50 basis points per month, which is basically where the size premium was at during its so-called "golden age" period before 1980.

To quote the paper again:

> *"Controlling for quality or junk fully explains the seemingly very different performance of the basic size premium over these two different periods."*

Controlling for junk revives the size premium internationally

Great news for the rational investor who realizes it's important to diversify by geography as well as by asset class.

It was thought that the size premium was largely a U.S. phenomenon. However, when controlling for quality and removing the junk, the size premium was positive in 23 out of 24 countries included in the study.

So, remember, friends don't let friends buy small-cap growth stocks with weak profitability.

What is the profitability premium?

Here is a mind-bending investment fact.

Highly profitable companies tend to make better investments than companies that lose money.

I know what you're thinking: that fact alone is worth the price of this book.

As established in a 2012 paper titled "The Other Side of Value: The Gross Profitability Premium", written by Robert Novy-Marx, the profitability premium is the inverse of the value premium.[58]

Novy-Marx defines the profitability premium as gross profits-to-assets. Despite having higher valuations, firms with higher profits relative to assets provide exceptional returns.

As we just discussed with the size premium, the real beauty of the profitability premium is its ability to enhance other factors. When we remove unprofitable, junky small-cap companies, the size premium is revived. Similarly, Novy-Marx found that controlling for quality also greatly enhanced the value premium.

What is the investment premium?

The final risk factor worth your time is the investment factor.

Larry Swedroe, Chief Research Officer at Buckingham Wealth Partners, provided an excellent rational explanation of the investment premium in a 2019 blog post[59]. To quote Larry:

> *"Rational theories suggest that the investment premium reflects firms' investment decisions—firms invest when they have low leverage and expected stock returns are low (the discount rate is low, making the net present value of the investment higher), whereas firms do not invest when they have high leverage and expected stock returns are high."*

58 Arnold, T. M. (2013). The Other Side of Value: The Gross Profitability Premium. CFA Digest, 43(2), 105–107. https://doi.org/10.2469/dig.v43.n2.56

59 Does leverage explain the investment premium? (2019, June 13). Alpha Architect. https://alphaarchitect.com/2019/06/does-leverage-explain-the-investment-premium/

Here's a simpler explanation of investment premium.

Imagine two companies that generate the same amount of profit.

- Company 1 achieved those profits while taking on $10 million in debt
- Company 2 achieved those profits while taking on $50 million in debt

All else being equal, company 1 will provide greater reliable returns to the investor over time. The company that has to invest more aggressively to generate the same amount of profits will be less likely to pass along those profits to shareholders, which is what we care about as investors.

The investment premium is defined as Conservative minus aggressive (CMA,) the difference in investment returns between companies that invest conservatively and companies that invest aggressively.

Returning to the example of the dreaded small-cap growth stocks with weak profitability, there is a good chance that these companies also invest aggressively and probably too aggressively in reality.

Is one factor premium better than another?

Let's talk about how the rational investor might take all this academic knowledge about factors and implement them in a portfolio.

One question that might come up is if it makes sense to favor one factor over another. For example, does it make sense to favor value over investment? Or size over profitability?

That's the question that Stanley Black and Wei Dai wanted to answer in their 2021 paper titled "Assessing the Relative Magnitude of Premiums."[60]

60 Black, S., & Dai, W. (2021). Assessing the Relative Magnitude of Premiums [Review of Assessing the Relative Magnitude of Premiums]. Dimensional Fund Advisors.

Black and Dai evaluated whether the size, value, or profitability premiums had different magnitudes within the U.S. or in international stocks from 1927-2020. They found no statistically significant differences in the expected premiums in the U.S. or international stocks over that nearly 100-year timeframe.

Based on these results, the rational investor would not favor one factor premium over another or one geographic region over another when implementing factors into a portfolio.

How do investors include factors in their portfolios?

Here's another important practical question that investors need to consider: does it make more sense to have multiple ETFs that target a specific factor premium or one ETF that targets all the factors at the same time?

That is the question that Dai et al. (2021) wanted to answer in their 2021 paper titled "Pursuing Multiple Premiums: Combination vs. Integration."[61]

As they explain in the paper, investors have two options to consider when implementing factors in a portfolio.

1. Adding multiple funds to an index-based portfolio that targets each factor individually. For example, a fund that targets the value premium, another fund that targets the size premium, etc. They call this a satellite approach to factor investing.
2. Adding one fund to an index-based portfolio that targets multiple factors simultaneously. They call this the integrated approach to factor investing.

61 Dai, W., Saito, N., & Watson, S. (2021). Pursuing Multiple Premiums: Combination vs. Integration. SSRN Electronic Journal. https://doi.org/10.2139/ssrn.3793594

Their results show that the integrated core approach can better account for the interactions among multiple premiums and lead to more reliable outperformance, better risk control, and lower costs to investors.

The difficulty in finding integrated factor funds that follow the research

The most difficult part of factor investing is also the more important: picking the right ETF to implement a factor strategy in a portfolio.

The financial services industry has read all of the research I have outlined in this chapter. They are aware of the expected outperformance of factor investing in the long run, and you can guess what they did with that information: create way too many "factor funds" or, as some fund companies market it, "smart-beta".

There is a massive variance in the quality and cost of the many factor funds out on the market.

This book aims to arm you with the knowledge to make evidence-based decisions, not give advice on specific funds to put your money in. That being said, the least I can do is point you in the right direction of investment firms that (at the time I write this) offer factor funds that follow the evidence and have reasonable investment fees.

The first is Dimensional. You may have noticed several papers in this chapter that were written by researchers at Dimensional fund advisors. They do fantastic research and even have Eugene Fama himself as a consultant.

The second is Avantis which offers factor ETFs similar to Dimensional.

If you feel factor investing is right for you, you might want to reach out to each of these firms and see how their factor funds stack up against each other and others in the market.

Does the rational investor include factors in their portfolio?

Factor investing adds complexity to a portfolio. Factor premiums can also be negative for years, leading to a situation where an investor with factor tilts in their portfolio underperforms the simple index investor.

Factor investing is not for the faint of heart and returning to our sundae analogy: factors are the cherry, not the sundae. Factors have an excellent use case when sprinkled on top of a portfolio of globally diversified index funds and held for the long term. Great care must also be taken to select the right factor fund that properly implements factor strategies in a low-cost way.

All of these caveats aside, from a purely rational perspective, the evidence is clear that including factor tilts in a portfolio increases expected risk-adjusted returns over the long run, which is the goal of the rational investor.

Part 3: Irrational Investing Mistakes and how to Avoid Them

In Part 1 of this book, I made the case for why index funds are the rational way to invest in stocks.

In Part 2, I reviewed the most popular alternatives to index investing you will be pitched throughout your investing career and discussed whether each had a place in the portfolio of a rational investor based on the best available evidence.

In part 3, I will wrap everything up by reviewing the most common irrational investing mistakes and how you can avoid them.

Part 3 is the most crucial section of this book because it's one thing to look at the evidence and agree that index investing makes sense. Sticking with a buy and hold indexing strategy is very difficult over a 40-50 year timeframe when there will be a lot of people constantly trying to scare you into selling at the worst possible time.

Most of these mistakes are driven by fear. The purpose of this final section of the book is to give you the data and tools you need to push back against the fear-driven narratives the financial media uses to hold your attention and sell ad space.

Chapter 26: How do you Lose Money with Index Funds? By Timing the Market

If most people were asked to name the biggest threat to their investments, they would probably say it is an economic recession or a financial crisis that leads to a stock market crash.

If you invest in low-cost index funds, you would be wrong: a stock market crash is not the biggest threat to your investments. **You are the biggest threat to your investments.** The easiest way for index investors to lose money is to try and time the market.

What is market timing?

Market timing is an investing strategy where investors move in and out of the market in an attempt to avoid losses and buy back in at the bottom after the market crashes.

Investors who time the market believe that they know what will happen in the stock market. Anyone who thinks that is delusional because no one knows what is about to happen in the stock market.

Someone trying to time the market would sell their stocks if they believed the market was about to crash. In doing so, they would avoid the pain of the losses that come with a market crash.

When the market has hit bottom, they would reinvest all of their money and ride the market back to the top and make themselves rich. It's the ultimate embodiment of "*buy low, sell high.*"

The idea of market timing is a great narrative, but when we begin to examine it closely, it becomes clear that it is nearly impossible to pull off in reality.

Market timing plays into our biases

Rational investors with a long-term investing horizon understand and accept that the stock market is incredibly volatile in the short run and very profitable in the long run.

Enduring the painful volatility in the short run is the price we must pay for the immense profits of investing in the long run.

But losing is painful, and the human brain is hardwired to avoid pain. We all suffer from "*loss aversion*".

We hate losing even more than we love winning. That leads people to make irrational fear-based decisions that they believe will help them avoid pain. As Master Yoda would say, "*Fear is the path to the dark side.*"

It's bad enough that the human brain is prone to loss aversion, but humans are also likely to be overconfident in our abilities. Many investors accept that market timing is generally a bad idea, but somehow they believe they are the exception to the rule. "*Market timing doesn't work for most people, but I am smarter than most people, and I have been studying the markets for a long time.*"

When you combine the biological urge to avoid pain with overconfidence, you can understand why so many investors try and time the market.

If you can't take the pain, you don't deserve the gains

Ask yourself why someone would invest in the stock market in the first place? The answer is obvious: investors put their money in the stock market because it offers superior expected returns compared to other investments.

The reason the stock market has such high expected returns is that it involves risk. **The higher returns are the reward for taking on risk**. The difference between stock market returns and a safe investment like Treasury bills is called the "risk premium".

The idea of market timing implies you can have the high returns from investing in stocks without taking on the risk. If it sounds too good to be true, it's because it is.

Recessions and market crashes are a fact of life. It's not a question of "*if*" you'll experience a market crash. The only question is "*how many*" market crashes you'll experience during your lifetime.

Remember, short-term pain is the price we pay for long-term gains and wealth building.

The risk of market timing

We already discussed the fairytale of market timing: you pull your money out right before the crash and get it back in the market before the recovery.

In reality, when many investors pull their money out of the market, they miss out on some of the market's best returns.

Merril Lynch researched what happens when investors try and time the market. They examined the return on a $1,000 investment in the S&P 500 from 1989-2018 under three scenarios.[62]

- **Scenario 1:** The investor implements a buy and holds strategy.
- **Scenario 2:** The investor pulls their money out of the market and misses the 10 best-performing months.
- **Scenario 3:** The investor pulls their money out of the market and misses the 20 best-performing months.

The results demonstrate the risk of market timing.

- The buy-and-hold investor ended with $17,306, a 1,631% return on investment.
- The investor who missed the 10 best-performing months ended with $6,959, a 596% return on investment.
- The investor who missed the 20 best-performing months ended with $3,328, a 233 % return on investment.

Volatility works both ways, there are periods of extreme negative volatility, but there are also periods of extreme positive volatility where the stock market goes through the roof in a very short period.

The risk of market timing is that you pull your money out, expecting the market to drop, and it soars upwards, and you miss out on those gains.

Successful market timing requires you to know two things

1. Exactly when to pull your money out of the market.
2. Exactly when to put your money back into the market.

62 Here's why time in market is more important than market timing. (n.d.). Merrill Edge. https://www.merrilledge.com/article/focus-on-time-in-market-not-market-timing

The odds of you successfully timing the peak and bottom of the market are extremely low.

A more likely scenario is that you would sell too early and buy back too late.

Keep it simple, boring and profitable

Investing involves risk. Trying to avoid this risk by timing the market simply opens you up to uncompensated risk. The risk premium for market timing is usually negative. Anyone who invests in the stock market needs to accept the fact that they will have years where their investments go down.

It sucks, but it's the truth.

Charlatans will try to make money off you by telling you the convenient lie that investing can be painless. The hard truth is that investing can be very painful at times.

If you can't accept that you are not cut out to be a DIY investor. There is no shame in that. It simply means you should hire a professional to help you manage your investments and avoid the temptation of trying to time the market.

Here's a comforting fact: the stock market has always rewarded long-term investors who have what it takes to ride out the market crashes and bear markets.

In the next few chapters, we will explore common situations in which you will be tempted to time the market.

Chapter 27: Should you Invest when the Market is at an All-time High?

"The market looks overpriced. I'm going to wait until the next crash before investing any more money."

How often have you heard some variation of that narrative in your life? Probably a lot.

People are drawn to simple narratives. And what can be more simple than saying when the stock market reaches an all-time high, you should stay away because "what goes up must come down."

Except, like with most simple investing narratives, it's dead wrong. All we need to do is examine the data to realize that investing in stocks when the market is at an all-time high has usually been a smart decision.

The U.S. stock market reaches "all-time highs" more than you think

What do you think is more likely in a year when the S&P 500 reaches an all-time high?

Option 1: A market crash takes place later in the year?

Option 2: The market sets 10 or more new all-time highs in the same year?

Your gut is likely telling you option 1 is correct because, as we've covered, the financial media has economic incentives to keep you in a constant state of fear.

The reality is that option 2 is correct. When the market sets an "All-time" high, it's much more likely to keep going up than come crashing down. have a look at this chart below, measuring how many days in a year the S&P 500 closed at a record high.

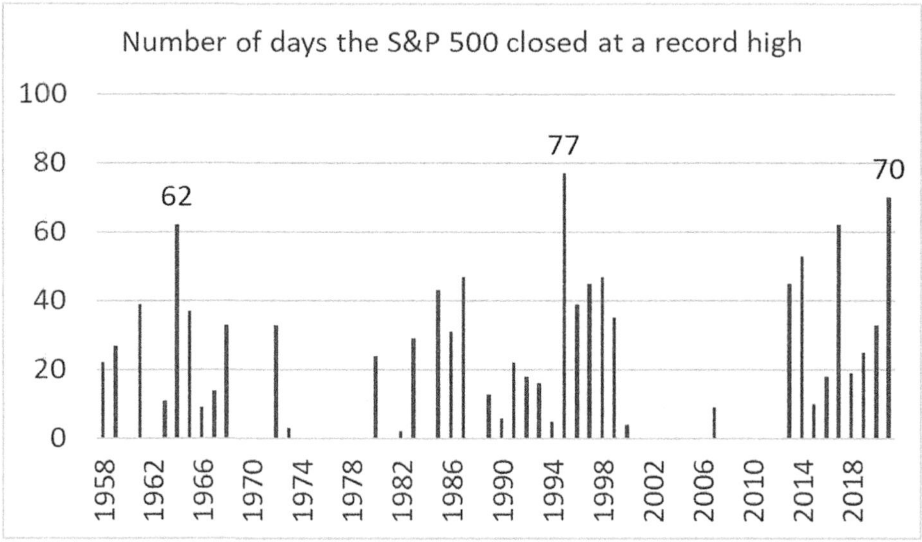

Data source: S&P Global, chart created by the author.

Here are a few facts about "new all-time-highs" that put this into context.[63]

- 6 out of 10 years since 1958 have seen multiple records in the S&P 500.
- Including years with zero new records, the market closed with a record-high 18-times per year on average.
- Excluding the years with zero new records, the market closed with a record high, an average of 29 new all-time highs per year.

Historically, in years where the market is going up, you would expect the market to set a whole lot of new records.

63 Essential Intelligence to Make Decisions with Conviction. (2018). Spglobal.com. https://www.spglobal.com/en/

Okay, so the market set's a lot of new records. But the big question is, how has the market performed AFTER setting a new all-time high? This question is important because it speaks to the narrative that by getting out of the market at an all-time high, you can outperform buy and hold investors who don't time the market.

How does the stock market perform after setting a new all-time high?

If a new all-time high is a sign of an impending market crash, as the pundits would have you believe, then we would expect investors who put new money in after an all-time high to lose money.

Except they don't.

Research from JP Morgan outlines the data that definitely shuts down the narrative that you should avoid investing your money when the market hits an all-time high.[64]

In their research, JP Morgan looked at the total S&P 500 returns from 1988 through April 2021 and found that if you had invested your money on a randomly selected day, your average return on investment after one year was 11.9%.

That's not bad at all. I'd take a 12% return any time.

But what would your average return have been if you only invested on days when the market closed at a time-high? 14.3%. **You would have outperformed by nearly 2.5% if you only invested after the stock market broke a new record.**

---

64 Top Market Takeaways | Is it worth considering investing at all-time highs? (2020). https://www.jpmorgan.com/content/dam/jpm/securities/documents/cwm-documents/Is-it-worth-considering-investing-at-all-time-highs.pdf

If we zoom out to a three or five-year time horizon, your cumulative returns from only investing after new all-time highs would continue outperforming.

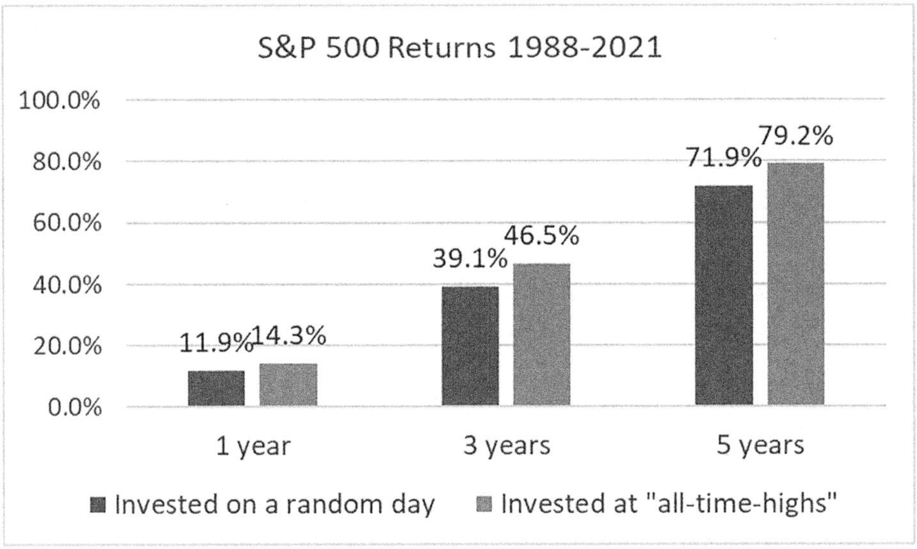

Data Source: JP Morgan, chart created by the author

Could it be that investing gurus who claim to know what's about to happen in the stock market are full of sh*t?

Stick to your plan

Does this mean a new all-time high means you should expect the market to keep going up indefinitely?

Of course not.

The kernel of truth that the pundits pushing the "wait for a crash" narrative exploit is that *eventually*, there is an all-time high that is followed by a crash or bear market. The problem is that we don't know if that will be in one day or 10 years from now.

It's simply more evidence that we should not time the market no matter how appealing the narrative of the day is. The lesson for long-term investors is to stick to your strategy and not get stressed about the fact that you're investing at an all-time high.

Chapter 28:
Buying the Dip is Market Timing With Better PR

Common advice when the stock market drops is to "buy the dip."

Buying the dip is when an investor invests even more than they normally would after the market has declined in value. It taps into the idea of "buy low, sell high."

While buying the dip is an infinitely better choice than selling the dip, if you're a long-term investor looking to maximize your wealth, you'll never allow yourself to be in a position to buy the dip.

Buying the dip is market timing with better PR

The rational investor does not "buy the dip" because they do not have investible cash lying around to buy when the market dips.

By "investible cash", I mean money that does not have a specific purpose in your financial plan. Cash in an emergency fund is not investible cash because the entire purpose of that money is not to be invested. Investible cash means leaving money aside as part of an intentional strategy to invest it after a market crash in hopes of higher returns.

Buying the dip is simply market timing by another name. Rational investors don't buy the dip because they don't time the market.

Let's say you had $10,000 in cash you could invest at the beginning of the year. You choose not to invest it because you feel the markets are overvalued, and a correction will come soon. Once the market drops, you will invest your extra cash.

Here's how that would have played out in 2021.

- From January to November, markets rose by 25%.
- At the end of November, markets dropped 2.5% on a single day.
- Pundits on Twitter made #Buythedip a trending topic.
- You decide this is the moment you've been waiting for, and you buy the dip by investing your $10,000.
- Congratulations, you bought the dip and cost yourself $2,188.

Had you invested $10,000 in January, it would be worth $12,500 before "the dip". After the dip, it would be worth $12,187.

This is a great reminder of the foundational truths of investing:

> *"Time in the market beats timing the market."*

When buying the dip gets dangerous

Holding cash aside to "buy the dip" has opportunity cost but probably isn't a lethal financial mistake.

One mistake overly aggressive or nervous investors make is to grab cash from wherever they can find it—including their emergency fund or even taking on debt—to buy the dip.

This can be outright dangerous.

The reason you keep cash in an emergency fund is not to earn optional returns; it's to be there as an insurance policy in case you lose your job. If you clear out your emergency fund to buy the dip, what happens if the market continues to dip?

If the "market dip" is the beginning of a prolonged bear market or economic recession, then you're going to see your portfolio continue to decline.

If you were nervous when the market dipped and you had an emergency fund, you'll be freaking out if the market dips further and you have no cash remaining.

Then what happens if you have a real financial emergency?

You're in a position where you're forced to "sell the dip", the exact opposite of what you intended.

This is why it's so important to have different buckets of money with clearly-defined purposes.

- The purpose of cash in an emergency fund is to sit there collecting dust.
- The purpose of cash in a portfolio is to grow and generate income.

Set clear rules for each bucket of money you have and never break them.

Remember, rational investors, don't leave piles of investible money sitting around waiting for the next dip.

Chapter 29:
Even in Great Years, the Stock Market has big Drops

Here are two contradictory truths about the stock market.

1. Most years, the market goes up.
2. Even in good years, it's usually a painful experience.

When the stock market has a bad day, week, month, or even quarter, it's tempting to think that the wheels are about to fall off, and a bad stretch is a bellwether for a prolonged bear market.

Volatility, and often extreme volatility, is the rule, not the exception to investing in the stock market. It's incredibly rare for the stock market to go up and to the right for an entire year without major dips along the way.

There is always drama.

Dimensional fund advisors put together some data that highlighted how there are significant drops in the market even in good years.[65]

The following chart shows the total return of the Russell 3,000 Index (approximation of the entire U.S. stock market) alongside the biggest dip within the same year from January 2002 to December 2021.

65 Do Downturns Lead to Down Years? (n.d.). Dimensional. Retrieved June 1, 2022, from https://www.dimensional.com/us-en/insights/do-downturns-lead-to-down-years

Year	Total Annual Return	Intra-Year Drop
2002	-22%	-33%
2003	31%	-13%
2004	12%	-8%
2005	6%	-7%
2006	16%	-8%
2007	5%	-10%
2008	-37%	-49%
2009	28%	-27%
2010	17%	-16%
2011	1%	-20%
2012	16%	-10%
2013	34%	-6%
2014	13%	-8%
2015	0.5%	-12%
2016	13%	-11%
2017	21%	-3%
2018	-5.00%	-20%
2019	31%	-7%
2020	21%	-35%
2021	26%	-5%
	Average Annual Return	**Average Intra-Year Decline**
	11%	**-15%**

Data source: Dimensional fund advisors. Chart created by the author.

For example, we can see in 2010 the market returned a very nice return of 17%. Looking back at it years later it's tempting to conclude that if the market returned 17%, it must have been pretty smooth sailing for the entire year.

Nope.

The market was down as much as 16% in that same year. In fact, 2010 was the year of the infamous "Flash Crash", where the Dow Jones lost 9% of its value in 1 hour. Even more amazingly, it recovered 70% of that loss before the end of the day.[66]

Looking at the returns from 2002 to 2021—a period which included 9/11, the dot com crash, the great financial crisis, and COVID-19—we see the market returned 11% per year. The market also had an average intra-year drop of 15% over that same period.

Volatility is inescapable and there is usually a scary narrative attached to the volatility. Someone is always giving you a reason to be fearful and sell—even if that's not in your best interest.

Looking at the returns year by year masks a lot of volatility, which is exactly why the rational investor thinks long-term: not in days, quarters, or even years but in decades.

The further you zoom out, the quieter the day-to-day noise of the market gets.

66 Flash Crash. (2019). Investopedia. https://www.investopedia.com/terms/f/flash-crash.asp

Chapter 30: Is Dollar-cost Averaging a Rational Investing Strategy?

The best time to start investing is right now.

If you have access to cash that you want to invest, there are two strategies you can take to invest it.

1. **Lump-sum investing**: Where you invest all of your investible cash immediately. If you had $10,000 to invest, you would invest the entire $10,000 right away.
2. **Dollar-cost averaging**: Where you slowly invest a certain amount of your investible cash over a pre-determined amount of time. If you had $10,000 to invest, you might invest $1,000 per month over a 10-month period.

You have probably read a lot of conflicting advice on which strategy is better. "*Better*" is a subjective term and most people would use the outcome rather than the thought process to determine which is "better."

I can tell you which strategy is the rational choice: it's lump-sum investing.

Dollar-cost averaging "feels" safe

Most of us only have money to invest every time we get paid. To be clear, investing every payday is not the dollar-cost averaging I am talking about in this chapter. If you invest everything you can the same day money gets deposited into your bank account that is not dollar-cost averaging, it's lump-sum investing that looks like dollar-cost averaging, often referred to as "forced dollar cost averaging". If you are investing every payday that is a very good thing and you should keep doing it!

The dollar cost averaging I am talking about in this chapter is when someone has a pile of cash, and rather than investing it right away, they slowly invest it into the market in equal amounts over a predetermined amount of time. Say your rich uncle passed away and left you $10,000. If, instead of investing the $10,000 all at once, you invested $1,000 per month for 10 months: that's dollar cost averaging.

There is only one reason someone would implement a dollar-cost averaging strategy: they are afraid.

They fear that they will put all of their money in the market, and then the market will crash. This situation does create a "behavioral risk", where the investor experiences so much pain from watching their investment go down that they sell at the bottom and lock in a loss.

Here's the thing. Whether you invest a pile of cash all at once or over a 10 or 12-month period, eventually, you face the same risk of a market crash. If you take one practical lesson away from this article, let it be this. If you aren't comfortable investing a lump sum all at once, that is a signal that your portfolio is probably too risky for you to handle. This is your brain telling you that you might need to rethink your entire asset allocation.

The simplest explanation why lump sum investing beats dollar-cost averaging

The expected value of stocks is always higher than cash. This must always be true. If the expected value of holding cash were higher than stocks, the stock market would implode. Framed differently, **why in the world**

would anyone hold stocks if they expected to make less money than holding cash?

This is a perfect opportunity to remind everyone how realized investment returns are calculated.

Realized returns= Expected returns + Unexpected returns.

- **Expected returns** are the forecasted returns for the stock market. As we just reviewed, the expected returns are always higher than the expected return of holding cash.
- **Unexpected returns** are what actually plays out in real life. They are unpredictable, highly volatile, and are what drive our realized returns.

Since we have no way of knowing what the unexpected returns will be going forward, we have to rely on our expected returns and our ability to absorb risk when making investment decisions.

Since the expected returns for stocks are always higher than holding cash, lump-sum investing maximizes our expected returns and is the rational strategy.

The data makes a strong case for lump sum investing

A 2020 paper written by Ben Felix examined historical data in Canada, the U.S, the U.K, Australia, Japan, and Germany and compared how often lump-sum investing outperformed dollar-cost averaging over a 10-year period.[67]

67 Capital, P. W. L. (n.d.). Dollar-Cost Averaging vs. Lump Sum Investing. PWL Capital. Retrieved June 1, 2022, from https://www.pwlcapital.com/resources/dollar-cost-averaging-vs-lump-sum-investing/

Here's the headline takeaway from the paper: **Lump-sum investing beat dollar-cost averaging 65% of the time across all the markets included in the study.**

On average, by implementing a dollar-cost averaging strategy, investors' returns were 0.38% lower per year over the 10-year period.

A 2012 research paper from Vanguard titled "Dollar-cost averaging just means taking risk later" examined the historical performance of lump-sum investing vs. dollar-cost averaging across three markets: the U.S, the U.K, and Australia.[68]

The Vanguard study examined the probability of lump-sum investing outperforming dollar-cost averaging in rolling 10-year periods going back to 1926 in all three markets.

- In both cases, the investor chose a 60–40 stock-bond allocation.
- The holding period was 10 years.
- In the dollar-cost averaging scenario, the investment was spread evenly over a 12-month period.

They found that for U.S, U.K, and Australian investors, lump-sum investing outperformed dollar-cost averaging 67% of the time.

The average outperformance over 10 years was 2.3% in favor of lump-sum investing.

The longer the dollar-cost averaging period, the more lump-sum investing outperformed.

---

68 Shtekhman, A., Tasopoulos, C., & Wimmer, B. (2012). Dollar-cost averaging just means taking risk later. https://static.twentyoverten.com/5980d16bbfb1c93238ad9c24/rJpQmY8o7/Dollar-Cost-Averaging-Just-Means-Taking-Risk-Later-Vanguard.pdf

Dollar-cost averaging offers less downside protection than you might think

At this point, you might be thinking, "*Yes, Ben, we know lump-sum investing beats dollar-cost averaging most of the time, but what I want is protection against a market crash.*"

If that's the case, then I have more bad news for you: dollar-cost averaging provides little downside protection.

The paper written by Felix examined lump-sum investing vs. dollar-cost averaging during the bottom 10% of scenarios where the market was historically bad. This is the exact situation for which dollar-cost averaging was created: to avoid the pain of being fully invested during a market crash.

The Felipaper found that in half of the countries examined (U.S, Canada, Australia), lump-sum investing still beat dollar-cost averaging even during historically lousy stock market returns.

They also examined lump-sum investing under two more scenarios:

#1 During a bear market.

After the market has dropped by 20% or more, lump-sum investing beat dollar-cost averaging 54% of the time, and added 0.25% per year to investment returns.

#2 When the market is at a "peak."

When market valuations are historically high and the market reaches a new record, you might see more investors engage in dollar-cost averaging to "avoid the crash". But the paper found that lump-sum investing outperformed dollar-cost averaging in these scenarios 64% of the time. This is consistent with the evidence we reviewed in Chapter 30.

To put it bluntly: **Dollar-cost averaging offers little protection from bad outcomes and is likely to cost you money.**

There's nothing to fear but fear itself.

If you are a rational long-term buy-and-hold index investor, you don't have much to fear from a market crash.

To drive that point home, consider what would have happened if you invested $10,000 into an S&P 500 index fund right before the four worst market crashes of the past 40 years and held on to today without adding any more money. This also assumes you reinvested any dividends received and is current as of April 2022.

February 2020: the market peak before the COVID-19 market crash.

- The market dropped by 34% in a matter of three weeks.
- Today, you would have $13,798 for an annualized return of 16%.

October 2007: the market peak before the financial crisis.

- The market declined by more than 50% over a year and a half.
- Today you would have $37,934 for an annualized return of 9.63%.

March 2000: the market peak prior to the dot-com bubble burst.

- The market dropped by 49%.
- Today you would have $45,745 for an annualized return of 7.13%.

October 1987: Prior to "Black Monday"

- The market dropped by a record-setting 20% in a single day.
- Today you would have $324,092 for an annualized return of 10.6%.

Many investors employ a dollar-cost averaging approach because they fear a market crash. As we have covered in this chapter, dollar-cost averaging likely won't do much to save you from a market crash.

If you can't stomach investing a lump sum today, what makes you think you'll be able to stomach it once you've finished dollar-cost averaging?

If you are too afraid to invest a lump sum, that is a signal that you are taking too much risk in your portfolio. Framed differently, we can say that the optimal level of risk you are willing to take in your portfolio is found when you can invest a lump sum without batting an eye.

Chapter 31:
The Stock Market is not the Economy

There's no shortage of scary investment narratives the financial media and stock market gurus will use to scare you into giving you their attention—and your money. Over the next few chapters, we will review what the data says about some of the most commonly recurring scary investment narratives.

One of those narratives is the "inverted yield curve". This is when shorter-term bonds have higher yields than longer-term bonds—which is the opposite of a "normal" yield curve where longer-term bonds have to pay more interest to get you to commit your principal for a longer period.

The reason you hear so much about an inverted yield curve when it happens is that an inverted yield curve has preceded every economic session since 1955.

Should you care about an inverted yield curve if you have money invested in the stock market?

Inverted yield curves are not an effective market timing tool

An inverted yield curve and the implication of a future recession is catnip to the financial media. Especially for stock market gurus who make their living pretending they know what is about to happen in the market and what moves you should make with your portfolio to stay ahead of the game.

When the yield curve inverts, many pundits will tell you it's time to start selling stocks, which makes intuitive sense. If the inverted yield curve implies an impending recession, why not dump your investments today to avoid a market crash in the future?

There are many reasons why a rational investor would avoid this kind of knee-jerk reaction, but let's focus on a specific reason: the stock market is not the economy!

A *possible* recession at some point in the future does not mean stock prices are about to plummet.

Fama and French take on the inverted yield curve

The question that should concern investors is, does it makes sense to sell stocks when the yield curve inverts?

To answer that question, let's turn to research from Professors Eugene Fama (University of Chicago) and Ken French (Dartmouth). In a 2019 paper titled "Inverted Yield Curves and Expected Stock Returns", Fama and French examined whether stocks underperform Treasury Bills (risk-free assets) when the yield curve inverts.[69]

Fama and French examined monthly data on stocks and bonds from the U.S. and 11 other major financial markets from 1975-2018.

They estimated the results of two investing approaches.

1. **A passive strategy** which consists of three separate stock portfolios: The entire U.S. stock market, the entire global stock market, and

69 Fama, E., & French, K. (n.d.). Inverted Yield Curves and Expected Stock Returns. https://famafrench.dimensional.com/media/467645/inverted-yield-curves-and-expected-stock-returns-july-28-2019.pdf

the entire global stock market minus the U.S. In the passive strategy, the investor applied a buy-and-hold strategy where they did not react to an inverted yield curve.

2. **An active strategy** where the investor sells stocks and buys U.S. Treasury Bills when the yield curve inverts.

Here is their research goal in their own words:

> *"To assess whether the expected equity premium—the expected return on stocks in excess of the T-bill return—is negative after an inversion."*

- If the risk premium is negative after the yield curve inverts, the active investor would outperform the passive investor.
- If the risk premium remains positive, the buy-and-hold passive investor outperforms the active investor who tries and times the market after the yield curve inverts.

So, which strategy provides better returns?

To answer this question, Fama and French constructed an active strategy that reallocated more of the portfolio to T-Bills for each month the yield curve was inverted in the prior 12-month period.

Since the passive strategy simply bought the whole market, the difference between the active and passive portfolio was the "active premium". A positive active premium means reallocating out of stocks when the yield curve inverted outperformed the buy and hold strategy. A negative active premium means buy and hold provided superior returns.

They examined returns in one, two, three, and five-year periods after the yield curve inverts.

Here's what they found

The U.S. and global passive investing strategies outperformed the active strategy of using an inverted yield curve to time the market in 24 out of 24 scenarios. The world index minus the U.S. outperformed in 19 out of 24 scenarios.

This means an investor who bought a total U.S. or global market index fund and did nothing when the yield curve inverted consistently outperformed the investor who sold stocks in response to an inverted yield curve.

Here's Fama and French's explanation of these results:

> *"The simplest explanation for the results is that inverted yield curves provide no information about future excess stock returns. If so, the negative realized premiums are the cost of uninformed bets against the equity premium."*

Put in the simplest possible terms: If you try to use an inverted yield curve as a market-timing tool, you're probably going to lose money.

Investing in a portfolio of low-cost, globally diversified index funds and sitting on them remains the rational decision whether or not the yield curve inverts.

Hopefully, this evidence can provide you some measure of calm the next time the investing pundits and gurus tell you the sky is about to fall because the yield curve just inverted.

Chapter 32: Should you Worry About Rising Interest Rates?

The financial media feasts on narratives about interest rates.

This is particularly true in rising interest rate environments where financial conditions tighten and investors get nervous. Endless hours of content are created by trotting out experts who all have different opinions on what rising interest rates mean for investors and if or when you should sell your portfolio.

All this commentary works under a few basic assumptions:

1. That rising interest rates automatically means stock prices will go down.
2. That you can prevent losses by listening to their advice.

Let's look at the evidence to see if these assumptions hold water.

Which "interest rate" are we talking about?

Specifically, the interest rate that impacts the stock market is the federal funds rate set by the federal reserve. The federal funds rate is the rate at which the federal reserve suggests banks borrow and lend money from each other.

Why does the federal funds rate matter?

The federal funds rate is important because it impacts the rate at which banks can borrow money and lend money. If the overnight rate rises, the cost of borrowing for banks rises. Banks will pass along this increased cost of borrowing to consumers and businesses to the extent they can.

Investors worry about rising interest rates because they fear that rising rates will lower the valuation of stocks. Put simply; investors worry rising rates will bring stock prices down.

What does the data say?

Researchers at Dimensional fund advisors looked at how U.S. stocks performed in months when the federal funds rate changed from 1983-2021.[70] There was a fairly even split in months where rates increased (70) to months where is decreased (67).

Here's how the stock market performed.

- Months where rates increased: up 1.05%
- Months where rates decreased: up 1.17%
- Months where rates did not change: up 1.02%

On average, U.S. stocks performed better in months where rates increased compared to months where rates remained unchanged. While months, where rates decreased, had the best performance, **these results provide strong evidence against the narrative that rising rates will automatically lead to lower stock returns.**

What about a longer period of rate increases?

70 Surprisingly Benign How Stocks Respond to Hikes in Fed Funds Rate | Dimensional Fund Advisors. (n.d.). Dimensional. https://www.dimensional.com/us-en/insights/surprisingly-benign-how-stocks-respond-to-hikes-in-fed-funds-rate

In their research, Dimensional also looked at the annual returns of U.S. stocks in the one-, three-, and five-year periods following three different scenarios.

1. No rate hike
2. One rate hike
3. Two consecutive rate hikes

Their findings should help calm your nerves next time you see a headline about how increasing rates will bring the market crashing down.

- In the one-year period, stocks performed the best after two-consecutive rate increases.
- In the three-year period, stocks performed better when there was no rate increase, but a second rate increase did not bring down returns any more than when there was only one rate increase.
- In the five-year period, stocks performed best when there was no rate increase and second best when there were two consecutive rate increases.

In all scenarios, the average return over the one, three, and five-year periods were reliably positive.

Is this data telling us that it's impossible for rising rates to materially impact stock prices?

No.

This is particularly true when rates rise at a faster pace than investors expected. Quickly rising interest rates can have a big impact on the stock market in the short term.

What this data tells us is that it's not a guarantee that rising interest rates will negatively impact stock prices. It also tells us that selling stocks in response to or in anticipation of an interest rate increase from the Federal Reserve, is an easy way to leave money on the table.

Finally we should note that even if rising interest rates are painful in the short-run, they can be helpful for long-term investors. As rates rise, the return on risk-free assets rise. Since stocks compete against risk-free assets for investor dollars, expected future returns should rise as well.

The rational, long-term index investor looks at this evidence and concludes that rising interest rates are not a cause to panic.

Chapter 33: Should you Sell Bonds When Interest Rates Rise?

Not all investing narratives try and convince you to sell your stocks. Some of these narratives want you to sell your bonds too.

"*When inflation and interest rates rise, bonds become a useless investment.*"

That is a narrative you'll hear quite a lot when interest rates begin to move up, or inflation is higher than expected.

The reality is a bit more complicated.

While the expected returns of bonds are lower, and when inflation is higher than expected, or interest rates begin to rise, that does not mean bonds are worthless.

Let's break down the basic math of how bonds work to understand why.

The basic math of bonds

A bond is a fancy term for a loan. When you invest in bonds, you are loaning money to either a government or a corporation. You make money in bonds in two ways:

1. Collecting interest payments
2. Selling your bond to someone else at a higher price

Most people understand that when you loan someone money, they pay you interest. Fewer people understand that with a bond you can sell that debt to someone else. That's why the price of bonds and interest rates move in the opposite direction.

If interest rates go up, new bonds that are issued will pay more interest than the bonds currently in your portfolio. Why would anyone buy your bond paying 3% when they can buy a bond with the same risk-profile paying 4%? They wouldn't; that's why when interest rates rise, bond prices drop because you need to sell existing bonds at a discounted price.

Remember, if interest rates go up, the price of existing bonds goes down.

That's why when we enter a period of rising interest rates, investors become justifiably worried that the bonds in their portfolios are going to drop significantly in value.

The not-so-basic math of bond ETFs

The rational investor embraces diversification in every asset they invest in, including bonds. For that reason, we will focus our discussion on investing in bond ETFs which allow investors to buy thousands of bonds at once. For example, Vanguards Total Bond Market ETF (not an endorsement of this fund) allows you to invest in 9,441 bonds in one ETF.

If you're invested in a bond ETF, here are the biggest factors to be aware of when interest rates move up.

1. The "duration" of the bonds in your portfolio
2. How much interest rates rise
3. How fast interest rates rise

"Duration" is a measurement of how many years' worth of interest payments you would need to collect to recoup your initial investment. If you invested $10,000 in a bond with a duration of six, it would take you six years of interest payments to be paid $10,000.

Let's go back to our example of Vanguards bond ETF. At the time I write this, the average duration of those 9,441 bonds is 6.8 years. You would need to hold that ETF for 6.8 years to be repaid your initial investment in interest.

The higher a bond's duration, the more vulnerable it is to a rapid rise in interest rates.

If interest rates rise by 1%, a bond ETF with a duration of 6.8 years would be expected to drop by 6.8% in value. Bond ETFs with long durations will likely have very poor short-term returns as interest rates rise.

That looks pretty grim for anyone invested in bonds in a rising-rate environment.

However, it may not be as grim as some pundits would have you believe.

Remember, a bond ETF holds all types of bonds with different durations. As interest rates rise, the older bonds with shorter remaining durations will expire, and new bonds will be issued at higher yields.

If rates rise slowly, that can soften the blow to bond ETFs as more of the older bonds expire and get replaced by slightly higher yield bonds. If interest rates quickly spike, it could be quite painful for bond ETF investors.

If you're a long-term investor with a 20+ year time horizon, you'll be able to weather painful short-term returns more easily because, in the long term, the old low-yield bonds in your ETF are replaced with higher-yielding bonds with higher expected returns.

Whether you are a stock or bond investor, we need to accept that we will live through periods of rising interest rates. It will be painful in the short term, but we need higher interest rates if we want higher future expected returns in the stock and bond market.

Bond ETFs still play an important diversification role in a long-term portfolio even if interest rates are rising. If the economy goes into a recession, interest rates can start to move lower again increasing the returns to bond investors.

The rational investor does not sell their bonds in response to a totally expected outcome like interest rates going up from time to time.

Buy and hold applies to bonds as much as it does stocks.

Chapter 34:
How War Impacts the Stock Market

Investing narratives like inverted yield curves and rising interest rates are trivial in comparison to geopolitical conflicts and wars.

This is an unpleasant topic to think about for obvious reasons, but as the data will show, as a long-term investor, you are going to live through many geopolitical conflicts in your lifetime. These conflicts can be scary, sad, and will have negative impacts on asset prices—making them a perfect cocktail of emotions that can lead to investors selling their portfolio at exactly the wrong time.

In this chapter, we review the impact wars, and other international crises have on the global stock market and the implications for long-term, rational investors.

Defining an international crisis

A 2005 study written by Henk Berkman and Ben Jacobsen titled "War, Peace and Stock Markets" studies the impact of 440 international political crises on stock prices over the period 1918-2002.[71]

That is a shocking number as it works out to 2.5 crises per month.

How do Berkman and Jacobsen define a crisis?

71 Berkman, H., & Jacobsen, B. (2006, February 1). War, Peace, and Stock Markets. Papers.ssrn.com. https://papers.ssrn.com/sol3/papers.cfm?abstract_id=885980

They use the definition created by The International Crisis Behavior databases.[72], which states three criteria an event must meet to be deemed a crisis.

1. A threat to one or more basic values
2. An awareness of finite time for response to the value threat
3. A heightened probability of involvement in military hostilities.

To quote the paper: "*An international crisis begins with a trigger that creates a foreign policy crisis for one or more states and ends with an act that denotes a qualitative reduction in conflict activity.*"

The impact of a crisis on stocks

Here's how a crisis typically plays out as it relates to the global stock market.

- In the first month, the crisis causes a large negative shock to stock prices as investors scramble to understand the scale and likely impact of the event.
- In the remaining months of the crisis, stock returns may turn positive again but remain lower than before the crisis.
- Once the crisis ends, stocks begin to recover

Berkman and Jacobsen found that, on average, a crisis reduces average monthly stock returns by 0.13 percent. But remember that there is an average of 2.5 crises per month, which implies that **the total impact of crises on stock prices is 0.33% per month or 3.9% per year.**

The amount of wealth lost due to global conflict and crises is staggering. Berkman and Jacobsen estimated that in the year 2000, a year free of international crises would be worth more than $1.4 trillion U.S. dollars to international stock market investors.

72 ICB Project. (n.d.). ICB Project. Retrieved June 3, 2022, from https://sites.duke.edu/icbdata/

At the start of 2021 world market capitalization was estimated at $106 trillion. **A year without global conflict in 2021 would have been worth $4.1 trillion.**[73]

These international crises also increase volatility in the stock market, which makes perfect sense because conflict makes the future less certain.

Berkman and Jacobsen found that the start of a crisis increases the volatility of the world stock market by more than 33%. Most of that volatility goes away once the conflict ends.

Violent conflicts have the greatest impact on stock prices

It should be no surprise that violent conflicts have the largest impact on global stock prices and market volatility. This is especially true when a major global power like the U.S. is involved.

Here are a few examples Berkman and Jacobsen cite to illustrate the impact of war and violent conflict on world stocks.

- 5% drop in world stocks at the start of the Gulf war in August 1990.
- 6% drop in world stocks in the month of the Slovenian-Croatian crisis in June 1991.
- 14% drop in world stocks in August 1998 when the U.S. embassy bombings took place.
- 9% drop in world stocks after the terrorist attacks on 9/11
- 11% in September 2002 at the start of the Iraq crisis that led to the invasion of Iraq by the U.S.

73 Capital Markets Fact Book, 2019 - Capital Markets Fact Book, 2019 - SIFMA. (n.d.). Www.sifma.org. https://www.sifma.org/resources/research/fact-book/

Another obvious conclusion is that markets react strongest to crises in their own country, with an average monthly loss of almost 1% compared to 0.4% for countries not involved directly in the crisis on either side.

Implications for rational investors

These results highlight that beyond the senseless human suffering of these conflicts, if humanity could better co-operate with each other we would all be much wealthier, safer, and more confident about the future.

The first thing to note is that this is even more evidence supporting the need to diversify globally and hold the entire world stock market. For example, U.S. investors would have been well-served to be globally diversified during the numerous conflicts their country has been involved with over the years.

Some crises are worse than others, but the sad reality is that with an average of 2.5 crises per month, the world has been living through a constant state of crisis to varying degrees.

Despite the constant state of conflict, the global stock market has continued to provide strong returns to investors through all of these crises. **A sad reality for humanity but a comforting note for investors that even violent conflicts have not prevented long-term, buy-and-hold index investors from earning strong returns and building wealth.**

Consider the following quote from Warren Buffett.

> *"Over the long term, the stock market news will be good. In the 20th century, the United States endured two world wars and other traumatic and expensive military conflicts; the Depression; a dozen or so recessions and financial panics; oil shocks; a flu epidemic; and the resignation of a disgraced president. Yet the Dow rose from 66 to 11,497."*

Chapter 35: Is Inflation Hedging Worth it?

So far, we have discussed some of the scariest investment narratives that the financial media, opportunistic investment advisors and online influencers will use to scare the rational investor into deviating from a passive buy-and-hold index strategy.

These narratives include economic recessions, rising interest rates, and even war.

But there is only one narrative to rule them all, and that narrative is inflation. There is no narrative that is used so blatantly to capitalize on the fear of investors and everyday consumers as inflation.

Whether you have money invested or not, we all feel the impacts when inflation is high. If inflation is higher than wage growth, quality of life drops.

When we experience higher than normal inflation, you'll read countless headlines like "The death of the dollar", "It's time to buy gold", or "Inflation is destroying your wealth."

So, how does the rational investor deal with periods of high inflation?

They do absolutely nothing.

Hedging for inflation is no easy task

One sub-narrative you will likely hear during times of high inflation is the different inflation hedges you should invest in to protect your money from inflation.

Without addressing any of the individual investments that are often marketed as inflation hedges, there is a fundamental truth that you need to know. **By the time high inflation has arrived, you have likely missed your opportunity to hedge against it.**

The closest thing to a true inflation hedge is likely Treasury inflation-protected securities (TIPS) issued by the U.S. government (or an equivalent real return bond in other countries). The principal of these bonds rises alongside inflation.

However, if you purchase TIPS ***after*** inflation has already spiked, then you lose the hedging benefit unless inflation continues to increase for a prolonged period.

TIPS are only an effective inflation hedge if you hold them in your portfolio before inflation spikes. This comes at a cost as TIPS generally have lower expected returns during periods of moderate to low inflation. This creates a drag on portfolio returns.

Rational investors don't hedge for inflation, they outpace it

A 2021 paper written by Wei Dai and Mamdouh Medhat titled "U.S. Inflation and Global Asset Returns" examined how inflation in the U.S. impacted returns for global asset classes, including bonds, stocks, factor premiums, commodities, and Real Estate Investment Trusts (REITs.)[74]

The study included nearly 100 years' worth of data and measured various asset returns during periods of low and high inflation in both nominal (before inflation) and real (after inflation) terms.

---

74 Dai, W., & Medhat, M. (2021, July 13). U.S. Inflation and Global Asset Returns. Papers.ssrn.com. https://papers.ssrn.com/sol3/papers.cfm?abstract_id=3882899

Here's the headline result that should calm any long-term investor worried about inflation:

Most assets had a positive real return during periods of both low and high levels of inflation.

Even with higher levels of inflation, investors were still making money. Inflation did not erode their wealth or destroy their portfolios. Inflation has historically been an unpleasant reality but nothing worth panicking about.

They did note that both commodities and energy stocks performed exceptionally well during periods of high inflation but that each of those assets are too volatile to act as an effective inflation hedge.

You are much more likely to lose money by tinkering with your portfolio in an attempt to avoid inflation than if you did nothing.

Bonds are the one asset class that is particularly vulnerable to inflation.

Dai and Mamdouh found that T-Bills had real average returns of negative 0.64% during high years of inflation. This makes sense when you consider what a bond is, which is an investment that pays a fixed income. So, higher than expected levels of inflation will eat away at the purchasing power of that fixed amount of income.

Global diversification may help cushion the blow of domestic inflation

Each country has its own rate of inflation. When you invest internationally, you get exposure to assets that are not directly exposed to the local inflation rate of your home country.

A 2014 paper written by Maximilian Rödel titled "Inflation Hedging with International Equities" found that international stocks could help blunt the impact of high domestic inflation.[75]

The paper stopped short of declaring international stocks as an inflation hedge and was found to be most useful in countries that had weak currencies. However, internationally diversified portfolios fared better than concentrated domestic portfolios during times of high domestic inflation.

Yet another reason to diversify by asset class and geography.

Does the rational investor hedge for inflation?

Not if they have a long investment horizon and a lot of human capital left.

True inflation hedges have to be held in a portfolio prior to periods of high inflation. By their design, true inflation hedges like TIPS have low returns during periods of moderate inflation, dragging down returns.

A rational long-term investor who has a portfolio diversified by asset class and geography does not need to hedge for inflation, simply outpace it.

Buy and hold remains the rational strategy.

---

75 Rödel, M. (2014). Inflation hedging with international equities. The Journal of Portfolio Management, 40(2), 41-53. https://doi.org/10.3905/jpm.2014.40.2.041

Chapter 36: Stock Market Crashes are Always Different, but the Result Never Changes

"*This time is different.*"

That's the narrative that dominates the news cycle when the stock market does experience a correction or even a crash.

Those who tell you that this time is different want you to believe that whatever is causing the current market crash will lead to a great depression-style financial catastrophe that will take decades to recover from—if we ever do at all.

As a rational long-term investor, the unpleasant reality is that you will almost certainly live through at least one major market crash in your lifetime. Any event with the power to crash the global stock market will be something that is genuinely terrifying. Think of a global pandemic or a financial crisis.

The next market crash will be your greatest test as a rational buy-and-hold investor. When that day comes, and every headline is telling you why "this time is different", I encourage you to return to this chapter.

As you are about to discover, the *cause* of every market crash is different, but the *result* is always the same: long-term index investors are rewarded for having the courage to do nothing when the whole world is screaming SELL!

What happens after a stock market crash?

What does the data and evidence say about stock market crashes? Are they ever really that "different"?

A 2018 paper written by William Goetzmann titled "Negative bubbles: What happens after a crash?" examined over 1,000 stock market crashes across 100 different stock markets from 1692-2015.[76]

Consider how extensive this dataset is: 100 global stock markets across 323 years. Compare that data to the blogger who declares "*this time is different*" next time we experience a major market crash.

Goetzmann defined a stock market crash as a 50% decline from a previous peak, which is exceedingly rare even by the standard of a market crash. During the great financial crisis, the S&P 500 dropped 46% between October 2007 and March 2009. So, if you are worried about a repeat of the financial crisis, the results of this study should be of great interest.

Goetzmann found that in the year after a stock market crash, the chance of a positive return was 60%. The market was more likely to be positive the year following a crash. The probability of an extremely positive return was much more likely than a second year of extremely negative returns.

In the year following a crash, stock markets were twice as likely to provide a positive 25% return than they were a negative 25% return.

Goetzmann referred to this increased probability of high positive returns following a crash as a "negative bubble". If it's the bursting of a bubble that causes market crash, a negative bubble is when the market quickly shoots back up to more normal levels

76 Goetzmann, W. N., & Kim, D. (2018). Negative bubbles: What happens after a crash. European Financial Management, 24(2), 171–191. https://doi.org/10.1111/eufm.12164

On average, a market crash prior year was associated with a 14.0% to 18.4% higher return.

Sadly for investors, they were less likely to be in a position to take advantage of negative bubbles because Goetzmann also found that investors were more likely to sell stocks after a crash and reallocate to less risky assets. In doing so, they turn paper losses into real losses and miss out on the rebound that follows a crash.

The legitimately scary narratives that are often associated with market crashes scare investors so much that they buy high and sell low, which is a sure-fire way to destroy wealth.

Rational long-term investors who hold onto their investments after a market crash are the ones who benefit from the negative bubbles that follow.

Interestingly, Goetzmann found that the negative bubble concept only applied to significant market crashes of at least a 50% decline from the previous peak.

Market corrections—declines in the 20+% range but less than 50%— were more likely to have further negative returns in the next year. This is what is called an extended bear market and will be the subject of the next chapter.

Chapter 37:
Extended Bear Markets is Where Future Wealth is Created

"*Don't invest money you can't afford to lose.*"

That's cliche investing advice that sounds smart but really only applies to people who either are under-diversified or invest in speculative assets.

Rational investors who think long-term and diversify properly should never expect to lose money. At least not permanently. There will be lots of volatility along the way, but diversified investors should never assume they are going to lose their money.

A better piece of advice is not to invest cash that you will need in the next few years. That's because stock markets can go into so-called "bear markets" that can last several years.

In broad terms, a bear market is described as a large decline in stock prices that persist for an extended period of time. The generally accepted definition of when a bear market begins is when a stock market index drops by at least 20% from its previous peak.

Long-term rational investors with lots of human capital left shouldn't fear a bear market. If you stay the course and keep investing, extended bear markets are an amazing opportunity to build future wealth.

A brief history of bear markets

The following table is a summary of the bear markets the S&P 500 has experienced since 1929 with data current to the date I wrote this chapter.[77]

Start Date	# Of Months	% Decline
Sept 1929	33	-86%
Mar 1937	62	-60%
May 1946	37	-30%
Aug 1956	15	-22%
Dec 1961	7	-28%
Feb 1966	8	-22%
Nov 1968	18	-36%
Jan 1973	21	-48%
Nov 1980	20	-27%
Aug 1987	3	-34%
Jul 1990	3	20%
Mar 2000	31	-49%
Oct 2007	17	-57%
Feb 2020	1	-34%
Average	**20**	**-39%**

The average of these bear markets lasted 20 months with a 39% decline. However, it should be noted that the length and severity of the "average" bear market are skewed by the two bear markets (1929, 1937) that took place during the great depression.

77 Franck, T. (2020, August 18). Here's a list of stock bull markets through time and how this new one stacks up. CNBC. https://www.cnbc.com/2020/08/18/heres-a-list-of-stock-bull-markets-through-time-and-how-this-new-one-stacks-up.htm l

The wealth-building opportunity bear markets provide

For a long-term investor, a long and painful bear market is the wealth-building opportunity of a lifetime.

In the chapter on market crashes, we learned what happens after a major stock market crash: future returns are elevated. Let's put some specific numbers to what these future returns look like. Here's how much the S&P 500 had to recover during each of the 14 bear markets.

% Decline	% Increase To Break Even
-86%	614%
-60%	150%
-30%	44.%
-22%	27%
-28%	39%
-22%	29%
-36%	56%
-48%	93%
-27%	37%
-34%	5%
20%	25%
-49%	96%
-57%	131%
-34%	51%

For example, to recover from the 1929 bear market which saw the S&P 500 drop 86%, the market increased by 614%. Every dollar invested at the bottom of that market would have increased by 614% by the time the market recovered.

The great depression is an extreme example, so let's use the most painful bear market in modern times, the great financial crisis which started in October 2007 and did not reach a bottom until March 2009.

To recover from that 57% drawdown, the market had to increase by 131% from its bottom. The market did not reach a new high until October 2013, a full six years from its previous high at the onset of the financial crisis.

During these six years, many U.S. investors were selling stocks, which, as we know, is exactly the wrong time to be selling.

Here's a hypothetical mental exercise to demonstrate what an amazing wealth-building opportunity anyone buying during this time got to experience.

- Let's say you started investing in March 2009 with a starting balance of $0.
- You invested $1,000 into an S&P 500 index fund until October 2013.
- Ignoring taxes and fees, you would finish with **$79,758.**
- If you kept that money invested and never invested another dime, by the end of 2021, you would have $252,851

The great financial crisis was an amazing wealth-building opportunity because it was a big crash with a slow recovery.

The problem with a big market crash followed by a fast recovery —like the one we experienced in 2020— is that it does not give investors much time to get new money into the market to take advantage of the outsized future gains when the market recovers.

If you are a rational investor, you don't have money sitting on the sidelines waiting for a market crash. When the market crashes, most of us are only able to get new money into the market every two weeks on payday.

The larger the drop and the slower the recovery, the more future wealth rational investors will build in an extended bear market.

Here's who should be nervous during a bear market

There are two groups of people that should be nervous during a bear market.

1. Stock pickers and speculative investors
2. Retirees

First, the stock pickers should be nervous because we know that throughout history, the market itself has recovered from every single bear market. The same is NOT true for individual stocks.

Some company stock prices will fall during bear markets and never get back up.

A stock market recovery does not mean every single company in the market will recover. Some stocks will do amazing, while others will continue to crumble. We have no idea which companies will fall into each category, which is one of the many reasons index investing is the rational choice to build long-term passive wealth.

Second, retirees have cause to be concerned about bear markets, even if they are index investors.

Why?

Because selling stocks to pay your bills at the same time, the market just fell 20%-60% is an easy way to outlive your money.

Think of the person who retired with $1 million in 2007 and then saw their portfolio drop to $432,000 during the 2007-2009 bear market. If they planned on withdrawing 4% of their original portfolio to pay the bills, they would have withdrawn an additional $60,000 over the 1.5-year bear market, leaving them with $372,000.

Yikes.

Of course, that is an extreme scenario and illustrates precisely why a retiree shouldn't be 100% in stocks. But the point remains: if you are at the point in your life where you are selling assets instead of buying them, a bear market can be scary.

Chapter 38: The Problem With "Investing in What you Know"

"*Invest in what you know.*"

That is a piece of investing advice you've likely heard before.

While it is important to educate yourself before investing your money, investing in companies in the same sector where you earn your income is an unnecessary risk. If there is a high correlation between your income and your investments, you could find yourself in a painful (and avoidable) situation where you lose your income and the value of your investments crash at the same time.

In this chapter, I provide a few common examples of situations in which investors connect their paycheck to their portfolio and why rational investors seek to minimize the correlation between their human and financial capital.

Taking company stock

A very common form of compensation at start-up and tech companies is having some or all of your compensation come through company stock rather than cash.

Let's say you're a software engineer at a tech start-up making $250,000 per year, and your only financial assets are stock in the company you work for. You are passionate about your company's mission, so you invest all of your money into the company. 100% of your human capital and financial capital are tied up in a single company. All your chips are on one number.

That looks pretty attractive during a bull market, and valuations for tech companies are rapidly expanding.

But as we discovered in the chapter of this book on factor investing and you realize that small, growth-oriented companies that are not yet profitable tend to fizzle out.

What happens if the start-up fails?

Your income and financial capital fall to zero.

How a rational investor working at a start-up would invest

The rational investor is not looking to get rich quick.

Instead, they want to "maximize their utility". That often means taking just enough risk to reach the desired outcome while attempting to minimize the odds of a negative outcome.

Here's how a rational investor working at a tech start-up would manage their finances to optimize risk-adjusted probable outcomes.

- First and foremost, the rational investor seeks to minimize the correlation between their human and financial capital.
- If they were offered the choice to be paid in cash or in company stock, they would opt for cash 100% of the time.
- An ultra-rational investor would likely take this a step further and might even take out a put option on the stock of the company they work for. This creates a kind of insurance policy that would further distance their human capital from their financial capital. In reality, nobody is actually that rational, and this is certainly not a recommendation to get involved in options trading.

The point is, that the rational investor always looks to minimize the correlation between human and financial capital whenever possible.

That means diversifying by geography and by asset class through a portfolio of low-cost index funds of stocks and bonds.

How correlated is your human and financial capital?

I use tech workers as an example because they often receive company stock as a core component of their compensation.

However, tech workers are not the only people who have their human and financial capital tangled up in a knot.

Think of the real estate agent who takes a portion of their commissions and invests in local rental properties. 100% of their income and their investments are placed on one bet: the local real estate market.

What happens if the local real estate market goes into a major correction?

- The agent will earn less commission
- The value of their rental properties fall
- The rent collected from those properties fall

All three of these things happening at the same time can be devastating for that real estate agent.

Or think of the small business owner who reinvests 100% of their profits into growing their business. They are "all in" with a single bet: their business.

What happens if their business fails?

They have no income and no financial capital to fall back on.

If you are an entrepreneur, I'm not advocating that you don't bet on yourself or invest in growing your business. But once your business starts generating a profit, put your rational hat on and start taking a small portion of those profits and investing in assets that have a low correlation with your business.

When it comes to managing your career and your finances, here's a rule of thumb: ***Invest your human capital in what you know and diversify your financial capital as much as possible.***

This allows you to be a good capitalist and a rational investor.

Investing your human capital in what you know maximizes your earning potential.

That's what it means to be a good capitalist.

Taking the money from your human capital and spreading it around in assets unrelated to your job or business helps you minimize the odds of being unable to pay the bills.

That's what it means to be a rational investor.

Chapter 39:
Investing With Leverage is Like Cooking With a Really Sharp Knife

Certain tools should be kept in the hands of professionals.

I learned this lesson the hard way when I bought my first industrial-quality chef's knife.

Do I need what amounts to a sword to chop onions and carrots?

No.

Did I almost cut my finger off several times and stain my cutting board with blood?

Yes.

A knife that sharp only needs to be wielded by a professional who:

1. Can use the knife to create dishes I can't and;
2. Has enough skill and experience to use it safely. If you've ever seen an experienced chef's hands, you'll notice all the scars; that's how they got their experience.

When it comes to investing, using leverage is a lot like using an insanely sharp chef's knife: it looks good on TV, but you'll probably end up cutting a finger off.

How does investing with leverage work?

Leverage is a fancy finance term for debt.

Using leverage simply means borrowing money to invest. Think of the real estate investor who doesn't have $600,000 in cash to buy a rental property, so they put up $100,000 and borrow $500,000 through a mortgage.

Although the mechanics are different, some stock market investors use debt for the same reason real estate investors do: so they can invest more and (hopefully) build wealth faster.

Let's go back to the real estate example.

You buy a $600,000 property using $100,000 of your money and borrowing $500,000. A year later, the property went up in value by 16% and is worth $700,000. A 16% return in one year is pretty great, but the story gets much better. Remember, you put up $100,000, and the property went up in value by $100,000, so your return on the money you used to invest is 100%.

The above is an example of how leverage can magnify your investment gains.

Here's another example with nice round numbers to crystallize this concept of levered returns.

- You buy a $1 million income property using $100,000 cash and $900,00 in debt.
- 1-year later, the property is worth $1.1 million—it went up 10%.
- Your levered return = 100% because ($1.1 million − $1 million) ÷ $100,000 = 1
- Or in more simple terms you put down $100,000 and the value went up $100,000 and since $100,000 = $100,000, you doubled the investment that you put down.

By the way, the reverse is also true: if the property went ***down*** by $100,000, your return would be negative 100%. You have a $900,000 property and $900,000 in debt, which means you have $0 in equity.

But wait, it can get much worse than that.

When you invest your own money, the worst you can do is lose 100% of your money. **When you invest with leverage, it becomes possible to lose more than 100% of your money.**

If you bought a $1 million rental property with $100,000 in cash and then the real estate market goes in the tank, and the property value gets cut in half to $500,000, you have a negative 500% return.

- You put up $100,000 and took on $900,000 in debt for a $1 million property.
- You still have $900,000 in debt, but now you have a property worth $500,000.
- Your levered returns are ($500,000 − $1million) ÷ $100,000 = -5 or -500%.
- You invested $100,000 to lose $500,000.

You'd be $400,000 underwater on that property. That means if you sold it, you would lose your original $100,000, plus you'd still owe an additional $400,000.

That's how you ruin your life or using my chef's knife metaphor, it's how you cut off your finger using a tool you had no business messing around with.

So far, we've used real estate as an example of how investors use leverage. Let's turn our discussion to using leverage to invest in stocks.

The rational case for using leverage to buy stocks

A 2008 paper written by Ian Ayres and Barry Nalebuf titled "*Life-cycle Investing and Leverage: Buying Stock on Margin to Reduce Retirement Risk*" makes the rational case for using leverage to invest in the stock market.[78]

They argue that young investors can achieve better "diversification across time" when they use leverage to buy stocks while they are young.

Remember, your total portfolio = human capital + financial capital.

- Young investors have a lot of bond-like human capital and very little financial capital.
- There is a rational case to leverage your bond-like human capital to buy stocks which will help balance out your total portfolio between bonds and stocks.
- As you get older, you have less bond-like human capital and you begin transitioning more of your financial capital away from risky assets like stocks and towards less-risky assets like bonds.

Ayres and Nalebuf used stock market data going back to 1871 to show that using leverage to buy stocks when young and "de-risking" a portfolio as you age provided superior outcomes in the past.

They found investors implying this type of strategy had 90% higher expected wealth in retirement compared to investors who use simple target-date funds and 19% more wealth compared to investors who were consistently 100% invested in stocks.

---

78 Ayres, I., & Nalebuff, B. J. (2008). Life-cycle Investing and Leverage: Buying Stock on Margin can Reduce Retirement Risk. SSRN Electronic Journal. https://doi.org/10.2139/ssrn.1139110

That additional wealth would allow investors to retire six years earlier or extend their retirement by an additional 27 years.

That is a very compelling case for young investors.

On the issue of buying stocks with leverage, I will make my first and only break in this book from the "rational" approach and caution against buying stocks with leverage.

While there exists a rational case for young investors to use leverage to buy stocks, this is the part where I must remind you that the concept of a perfectly rational investor is an impossible standard to achieve. We can all strive to be as rational as possible but none of us will be 100% rational 100% of the time. It's not in our nature as humans.

As I am about to make clear, the consequences of even a single moment of irrational behavior when using leverage to buy stocks can be devastating.

The dangers of using debt to buy stocks

If using leverage in real estate is like me using a razor-sharp chef's knife, using leverage in the stock market is like me handing that chef's knife to my two-year-old.

It's probably going to end badly.

For almost everyone reading this, it's probably a bad idea to use leverage to invest in the stock market. There are two reasons this is true.

1. The stock market is more volatile than real estate, and that volatility is much more visible.
2. Stocks are a very liquid investment.

Let's explore both of these issues in detail to paint a picture of how dangerous it can be.

Debt + Volatility = Disaster

We all know the price of stocks can swing up and down by very large amounts in a short period of time.

It's not the volatility of stocks that is the real problem; it's your awareness of that volatility that leads to bad investment outcomes. The volatility of stocks is right in your face. You can open up your phone and see the change in the value of your investment portfolio second by second.

When you invest in real estate, the price of your real estate assets could be just as volatile as stocks, but there is no electronic ticker on your phone showing you how the value of your property is changing second by second. If you want an updated value of your property, you need to do deep market research or pay an appraiser to do it for you.

Here's a four-step explanation of why the visible volatility of stocks makes them a bad investment to use leverage.

1. Visible volatility leads to panic.
2. Panic leads to selling when stocks are down.
3. Selling when stocks are down locks in losses.
4. If leverage was used, those losses would be compounded and irreversible.

It only takes a few seconds to liquidate a stock portfolio

The visible volatility of the stock market wouldn't be as big of a problem if it weren't so easy to sell off your entire portfolio with the click of a button.

The reality is you can sell off your entire portfolio with a click. So, if you see the market drop suddenly and sharply and you have a moment of panic, that moment of irrationality is all it takes to dump your entire portfolio.

Compare that to real estate. It's a much less liquid asset, so you can't sell it off in a few clicks. It takes weeks or months to sell a property and usually involves advisors like real estate agents who might be able to talk you out of selling at the worst possible time.

The temptation to use leverage to invest is enticing. It's the fastest way to build wealth, but it's also the fastest way to destroy wealth. On paper, it might make sense for long-term investors to boost their returns with leverage. But, in reality, most of us would end up cutting our own fingers off.

Chapter 40: Stoic Alpha: How Philosophy can Help Rational Investors Stay the Course

Trying to be a "great" investor is a self-defeating prophecy.

The rational investor knows that the more you tinker with your portfolio by picking individual stocks, selling stocks before an "*inevitable*" market crash, or getting into "*alternative*" assets, the worse your portfolio performs.

The data is clear on what happens to most investors who tinker.

- They have no idea when to sell the individual stocks they bought.
- They sit on the sidelines, waiting for that market crash that takes a lot longer than they ever imagined.
- Then when the market finally does crash, they wait too long to get back in and miss some of the best days in the history of the stock market.
- Their alternative investments underperform.

Most people would be better off simply sitting still and doing nothing through a market crash and recovery than tinkering with their portfolios ahead of time.

The more you do to avoid a bad investment outcome, the faster you bring about what you sought to avoid.

We are all myopic investors

A 1997 paper written by Richard Thaler et al. discussed how myopic loss aversion impacts investors.[79] They define myopic loss aversion as "*greater sensitivity to losses than gains and a tendency to evaluate outcomes frequently*".

They point to two behavioral traps that investors fall victim to.

1. **Loss aversion**. People hate losing more than they like winning.
2. **Mental accounting**. The narrow framing of current decisions and past outcomes leads to short-term rather than long-term thinking and constant evaluation of gains and losses.

Combine loss aversion with narrow mental accounting, and you get a myopic investor: someone who will constantly check their portfolio and feel deep pain when their portfolio is down.

Given the volatility in the stock market, the more you check your portfolio, the more often you will see your portfolio having a bad day. Of course, the number of good days will outnumber the bad days over the long run, but the myopic investor tends to forget the good days and hold onto the bad days.

They found that myopic investors will be more willing to take on more investment risk if they check their portfolio returns less often. Put another way, **myopic investors who constantly check in on their portfolios take on less investment risk, have lower exposure to the risk premium provided by stocks, and make less money**.

79 Thaler, R. H., Tversky, A., Kahneman, D., & Schwartz, A. (1997). The Effect of Myopia and Loss Aversion on Risk Taking: An Experimental Test. The Quarterly Journal of Economics, 112(2), 647-661. https://doi.org/10.1162/003355397555226

No matter what we tell ourselves, we are all, to some degree, myopic investors. The sooner we accept that fact, the sooner we can address the problem.

It's never been easier to slip into the bad habits of the myopic investor for two reasons.

1. We have a constant barrage of information about what's happening in financial markets from 24-hour cable news and social media.
2. It's never been easier to access and make changes to your portfolio. Just pull out your phone, and within a few seconds, you can make a potentially devastating financial decision.

Stoic alpha

Ryan Holiday's book "The Daily Stoic" opens with the following quote from the Greek philosopher Epictetus.[80]

> *"The chief task in life is simply this: to identify and separate matters so that I can say clearly to myself which are externals not under my control, and which have to do with the choices I actually control. Where then do I look for good and evil? Not to uncontrollable externals, but within myself to the choices that are my own..."*

If Epictetus were alive today, he would be an outstanding investor. Not because he would possess exceptional investment skills that would allow him to "*beat the market*". Epictetus would be a great investor because he would be wise enough to never try and beat the market in the first place.

80 Daily Stoic. (2018, July). Daily Stoic | Stoic Wisdom for Everyday Life. Daily Stoic. https://dailystoic.com/

Stoics would not view a stock market crash as inherently "*bad*". What is bad would be to let fear of a potential market crash in the future impact their investment decisions today.

When it comes to investing, wisdom is more important than skill.

Epictetus and those who practiced stoicism would achieve what I call "*stoic alpha*".

Generally, investment "alpha" refers to excess returns above the average market returns that are achieved through actively managing a portfolio.

Stoic alpha is the amount of money an investor does not lose because they have the wisdom to not pursue alpha in the first place.

All investors face the difficult task of tuning out the constant stream of information about what's happening in the stock market every five minutes.

Epictetus was fortunate that Twitter and 24-hour news cycles did not exist in his time. These modern forms of instant communication can make it difficult to achieve stoic alpha.

The simple but difficult task for a myopic investor would be to go on a financial media diet. While I am no philosopher, I do know that the easiest way to stick to a diet is to remove the junk food from the fridge.

Delete the stock market ticker from your phone. Take a break from social media—especially during volatile times in the market.

When you do engage with financial media, ensure you find writers and thought leaders who steer away from hysteria and lean into evidence-based rational thinking.

Understand that what happens in the market is outside of your power to control. The only decisions you can control as an investor are how you allocate your capital, when you choose to buy and when you choose to sell. Often, the wisest course of action is to do nothing.

Chapter 41: The Magic of Compound Interest Happens at the End

Throughout part 3 of this book, I have presented you with dozens of academic papers that lead to the simple conclusion that you should not sell your portfolio in response to the scary investment narrative of the day.

In this chapter, I want to illustrate the reward investors can expect if they have the discipline to start investing early and never sell until retirement.

Here are a few assumptions in a hypothetical situation.

- You have a 40-year investment horizon.
- Every month you invest $500.
- Your average annual return on investment is 8%.

If you never deviate from that plan after 40 years, you would have $1,745,503.

That's an eye-catching number. But any buy-and-hold investment strategy looks amazing when you zoom out 40 years. But early on, it's a lot of hard work, and it takes years before you start to see a major payoff.

Consider the following chart, which plots your total contributions, return on investment, and portfolio balance over those 40 years.

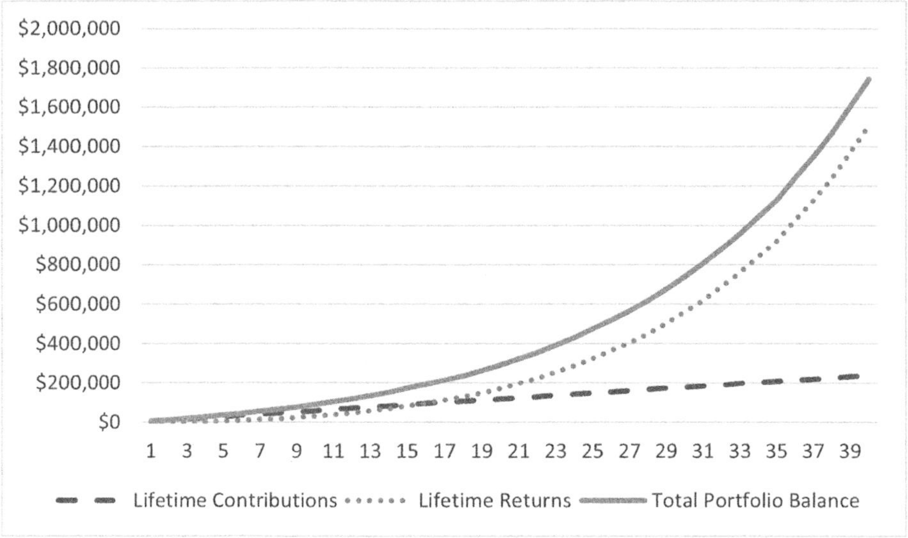

The first thing I want you to understand is that it isn't until year 16 that your lifetime return on investment (the dotted line) exceeds your lifetime contributions (the dashed line). That is more than a decade and a half of you doing all the heavy lifting.

From that point on, compounding begins to work its magic. Each year, more of your total portfolio value comes from investment returns, and less of it comes from money you contributed.

Here's a table that highlights how much of the wealth-building burden falls on you early on and how light the load gets over time.

Year	Contributions		Investment Returns	
1	$	6,000	$	225
10	$	6,000	$	7,276
20	$	6,000	$	24,078
30	$	6,000	$	61,373
35	$	6,000	$	94,620
40	$	6,000	$	144,153

In year one, you saved $6,000 and got a measly $225 return on investment. In year 40, you saved $6,000 and got an incredible $144,153 return on investment in a single year.

Of the $1,745,503 you have after 40 years, $240,000 came from your contributions and $1,505,503 came from investment returns. **Of that $1.5 million in investment returns, $940,324—or 62% of your total investment gains—comes in the final 10 years of that 40 year period.**

The magic of compound interest is at the end.

Warren Buffett's long-time business partner Charlie Munger once said, "*The first rule of compounding: Never interrupt it unnecessarily.*" I would change that quote to read, "*The first rule of compounding: It only works if you don't interrupt it.*" In fact, that is literally all you need to know about compounding. The longer you let compound interest work uninterrupted, the wealthier you are likely to become.

The next time a financial bullshitter tries to convince you to sell your portfolio of index funds before you planned—whether it be to get in on a trendy new investment or avoid an "impending market crash"— steel your nerves by reminding yourself of two facts:

1. This person likely has no idea what they are talking about.
2. By simply doing nothing, you will reap the rewards of compound interest.

Chapter 42: Stick the Landing: A Rational Approach to Wealth Decumulation

As the great Mike Tyson once said:

> *"Everyone has a plan until you need to start withdrawing from your portfolio without a paycheck."*

Of course, that is not the actual quote, but Tyson's point applies to a very important financial reality we all have to deal with. Creating a financial plan in a spreadsheet is easy. Following through on that plan and pinning your quality of life in retirement to that plan takes a tremendous amount of courage and unwavering belief in the plan.

When paychecks stop coming in, financial planning gets scary

Saving for retirement in your 30s is an intellectual exercise.

Executing the plan in your 70s is an act of faith.

- You make a plan (ideally) in your 20s or 30s, knowing you don't have to execute the plan for another thirty or forty years.
- A portion of every paycheck gets siphoned off to a retirement account.
- The whole process runs on autopilot, and you basically forget about it.
- Until one day, the paychecks stop coming in, and it's time to execute the plan.
- That's when it dawns on you: executing the plan means slowing spending down the nest egg you spent your entire life building.

- You've read all kinds of books and articles about *how to save for* retirement, but you quickly realize nobody ever told *you how to spend in* retirement.

That's when fear and panic kick in.

The rule of thumb that looks good on paper

I'm a fan of financial rules of thumb, but only if they are used properly.

Rules of thumb can be effective educational tools. They help take a very complex problem—like how to live off your savings for 30 years—and boil it down into a very simple concept.

To help people with the complex problem of living the lifestyle they want in retirement without running out of money, we have the 4% rule.

According to the 4% rule, you could withdraw 4% of your retirement savings to pay for your cost of living in retirement. If you had $1 million saved, you would withdraw $40,000 in year one of retirement and then increase that by the level of inflation each year.

The origins of the 4% rule can be traced back to a 1994 paper in the Journal of Financial Planning by William Bengen.[81] In his study, Bengen used U.S. data and built a hypothetical portfolio of 50% stocks-50% bonds to find the highest *sustainable* withdrawal rate for a 30-year retirement.

To do this, Bengen modeled the returns of this portfolio for every 30 years from 1926 to 1992. **He found that a 4% withdrawal rate was the maximum safe withdrawal rate for a 30-year retirement.**

---

81 Bengen, W. (n.d.). *ETERMINING WITHDRAWAL RATES USING HISTORICAL DATA*. https://www.retailinvestor.org/pdf/Bengen1.pdf

In 1998, a second study known as *"the Trinity study"* (named after Trinity University, where the study was done) found similar results as Bengen.[82] The Trinity study found that a 4% withdrawal allowed retirees a 95% chance of not running out of money.

Rules of thumb are a good place to start but a terrible place to stop learning about finance

Like any rule of thumb, the 4% rule is an oversimplification of a complex issue and fails to address many of the very real problems. Here are a few of the assumptions and limitations of the 4% rule.

- **It's not a flexible plan**. The 4% rule advocates you increase your spending each year by the rate of inflation regardless of what is happening in the economy or financial markets. It fails to deal with questions like what if inflation is 8%? What if the market goes down 50%?
- **It's modeled using a 50/50 portfolio of U.S. stocks and bonds**. That is a very specific asset allocation that does not include global diversification.
- **It relies on historical U.S. market returns**. Past returns do not imply future returns. At the time I write this, interest rates are historically low, which means expected future stock and bond returns are lower than in the past.
- **It assumes a 30-year retirement**. The 4% rule fails to answer questions like what happens if you retire at 65 and live to be a 110?
- **It ignores taxes and investment fees.** This is a perfect example of how a plan can look better in a spreadsheet than in real life.

---

82 *https://www.aaii.com/files/pdf/6794_retirement-savings-choosing-a-withdrawal-rate-that-is-sustainable.pdf.* (n.d.). Www.aaii.com. Retrieved June 8, 2022, from https://www.aaii.com/files/pdf/6794_retirement-savings-choosing-a-withdrawal-rate-that-is-sustainable.pdf

This highlights the limitations of financial rules of thumb, like the 4% rule. It's a helpful way to ease your way into the topic of withdrawal rates in retirement, but it should be the beginning, not the end of your research into this topic.

The only evidence you need to illustrate the limitations of the 4% rule is that its creator does not follow the 4% rule in his own retirement plan.[83]

Why it's difficult to execute any withdrawal strategy

We know two things to be true about the stock market.

1. In the long run, it goes up.
2. It doesn't go up every year.

The volatility of the stock market is not such a big problem when you are still working and have a paycheck coming in every two weeks.

But once you reach retirement and your only source of income is your portfolio, it becomes more difficult to fully trust in the models and projections that try and assure you everything will be alright in the long run.

There are limitations to the human brain's ability to remain rational.

More importantly, feeling uneasy about blindly trusting a rule of thumb like the 4% rule is not irrational. It's a sign you are aware of the very real risks such a simple plan presents.

Let's focus on the risks that a rigid withdrawal strategy presents.

---

83 Opinion | Not So Easy to Follow the 4% Rule in Retirement. (2022, April 26). *Wall Street Journal.* https://www.wsj.com/articles/retirement-planning-four-percent-rule-ben-gen-investment-11650923000

Sequence of returns risk: what if you have bad luck?

Historically, the U.S. stock market has gone down 4 out of every 10 years.

Again, not a problem when you're working.

But what happens if the market drops—potentially a lot—in the first year, you start withdrawing 4% of your portfolio?

Financial experts have labeled this "sequence of return risk".

- During your working years, if the market drops, it's an opportunity to buy.
- When the market drops in retirement, not only can you not buy, you are forced to sell.
- If the market drops in your first few years of retirement and you continue selling to fund your lifestyle, by the time the market recovers, you may not have enough left to fully enjoy that recovery. This puts your retirement in jeopardy.

Let's put some numbers to what this might look like.

Let's say you retire with $1 million invested in a 50/50 portfolio of stocks and bonds and you plan on using the 4% rule and sell $40,000 worth of assets in year one of retirement.

Then, out of nowhere, the stock market crashes, and your portfolio loses 30% of its value a few months into your retirement. Add in the $40,000 you withdrew to fund your retirement, and after one year, your $1 million retirement nest egg is down to $660,000.

In the first year of retirement, 34% of your nest egg is gone.

In year two, you increase that $40,000 withdrawal by the rate of inflation, and you keep increasing that withdrawal by the rate of inflation in each subsequent year. The longer it takes for markets to bounce back, the less savings you have left.

Sequence of returns risk is the risk that you get unlucky, and your investments perform very poorly in your first few years of retirement.

Longevity risk: what if you live too long?

A thought that only an actuary would have.

But a concern when living off a portfolio of investments is how long you think you'll live. The 4% rule was modeled on the assumption that your retirement lasts 30 years. Each subsequent year you live increases the risk of running out of money.

The *good news and the bad news* is that people are living longer.

Here's some data from the U.S. Census Bureau.[84]

- In 1960 the average life expectancy was 69.7 years.
- By 2015 the average life expectancy increased to 79.4 years.
- By 2060, the projected life expectancy is 85.6 years.

Longevity risk is magnified by sequence of return risk. If you plan on a 45-year retirement and the market crashes in your first year of retirement, the odds that you will outlive your money will skyrocket.

Inflation risk: what if my purchasing power goes down faster than expected?

84 Medina, L., Sabo, S., & Vespa, J. (2020). *Population Estimates and Projections Current Population Reports*. https://www.census.gov/content/dam/Census/library/publications/2020/demo/p25-1145.pdf

Here's another problem with a rigid withdrawal rule: you must make assumptions in your 30s about the inflation rate in your 70s and 80s. Which, of course, is unknowable.

Most retirement calculators and financial planners assume a constant 2% or 3% inflation rate. But what if inflation is higher when you reach retirement?

Here's how much $100,000 is worth in real terms after 30 years under various inflation rates.

- 2% → $55,207
- 4% → $30,832
- 6% → $17,411

The rational investor knows that **the stock market has a decent track record of outpacing inflation, but bonds do not**. The more bonds you have in your portfolio, the more a higher than expected inflation rate will destroy your wealth. A 50/50 portfolio (which the 4% rule is modeled on) is exposed to the risk of higher than expected inflation.

Allocating more of a portfolio to stocks can help address inflation risk, but that increases sequence of return risk given the volatility in the stock market.

Pick your poison.

What you need is guaranteed income in retirement

Guaranteed income is income you will not outlive.

Defined Benefit pensions are a great example of risk-free retirement income. So are government programs like Social Security in the U.S. or the Canada pension plan in Canada.

If you have enough guaranteed income in retirement to cover your essential spending needs, you don't need to worry so much about sequence of return or longevity risk.

Guaranteed income is like having a very secure paycheck in retirement. This allows you to take a rational long-term approach to your portfolio in retirement.

- If the stock market crashes in year one of retirement, it's no big deal because you have enough guaranteed income to ride out a bear market.
- If you live to be 125, you don't have to worry about eating cat food in your final years because you have guaranteed income that lasts as long as you do.
- In an ideal scenario, you're guaranteed income accounts for inflation, so you don't need to worry about loss of purchasing power.

If you don't have a Defined Benefit pension, you can use some of your financial assets to buy one.

How is this possible?

By using one of the most-hated but rationally sound financial products: annuities.

What is an annuity?

An annuity is a contract between you and an insurance company in which you make a lump-sum payment in exchange for a series of guaranteed monthly payments.

As part of the terms of the agreement, you can specify how long you want those payments to last.

- If you believe you will only live for another 25-years, you buy an annuity that pays you every month for 25 years.
- If you think you'll live for a very long time, you can buy an annuity to pay you every month until you die.

The longer you want guaranteed income to last, the more expensive the annuity will be.

People have written entire books on annuities, so it's beyond the scope of my work to dive into all of the nuances and complexities of annuities—of which there are plenty. The details of the contacts and the fees involved can vary significantly.

Dealing with issues like annuities is where a fiduciary financial advisor is worth their weight in gold (or better yet, in globally cap-weighted index funds). I can't stress enough how important it is to find an advisor who is looking out for your best interest when thinking of an annuity. The devil is in the details of the contract when it comes to annuities. It is not a decision that should be taken lightly.

Why economists love annuities

Annuities are largely ignored by the general public—and most people who know what an annuity is don't like them. So naturally, economists love annuities.

Economists love annuities because what economists want to do is minimize the risk of a retirement plan failing. Guaranteed income can help minimize sequence of return and longevity risks. If an annuity increases with inflation, all the better.

A lifetime inflation-adjusted annuity that covers your basic living expenses is an extremely rational approach to retirement.

If you know that all of your basic needs will be taken care of, you have the security and confidence to manage the remainder of your portfolio like a long-term rational investor.

In the same way, a 30-year-old with a secure paycheck every two weeks can stay invested during turbulent markets, so can a 70-year-old with a guaranteed monthly income.

To be clear, buying guaranteed income can be quite expensive.

Think of an annuity-like an insurance policy. Any insurance policy is simply transferring a particular risk to an insurance company. For example, with home insurance, you pay a premium and, in exchange, transfer the risk of your house burning down to an insurance company.

Annuities are no different. You pay the insurance company, and in exchange, you get to transfer sequence of return and longevity risks to the insurance company.

Whether you are buying car insurance, life insurance, or an annuity, all you are doing is paying a company to take certain risks off your plate and putting them on theirs.

Buying an annuity comes with opportunity costs

The first is the lost growth potential of your portfolio. Trading in a large portion of your retirement nest egg in exchange for guaranteed income means you won't accumulate as much wealth if financial markets perform great during your retirement.

An obvious implication of dying with less wealth means you will have less of a financial inheritance to leave behind.

Annuities are simply a tool to manage risk.

You do not have to trade in all of your assets to buy one. Depending on your level of wealth and the amount of guaranteed income you want in retirement, you could trade in anywhere between 1% to 100% of your financial wealth.

Having a baseline level of guaranteed income and leaving the remaining portion in a diversified portfolio to grow in the future is a rational way to manage risks, ensure you enjoy the retirement you've worked for, and still leave behind a financial inheritance.

A rational retirement plan is a flexible retirement plan

The future is unknowable which means that we must be able to adapt to whatever life or financial markets throw our way,

Retirement is simply a matter of how much you're spending and how much income you have coming in to fund that spending. A truly flexible retirement plan would allow you to adjust both your spending and income up and down as circumstances dictate.

Let's start with the importance of having variable spending plans in retirement.

This is something that financial planner, Micheal Kitces writes about quite a bit.[85] A variable retirement spending plan means adjusting your spending in response to what happens to your portfolio.

Let's return to sequence of returns risk, the situation where the market tanks and crushes your portfolio in the first few years of retirement. Your portfolio gets liquidated even more if you follow an inflexible plan like the 4% rule which tells you to keep withdrawing the same amount of money, regardless of what's happening in the market.

A variable spending plan can help alleviate some of the pressure caused by sequence of return risks. With a variable spending plan, you would adjust the amount you withdraw based on what happens in the market during the first decade of retirement.

If the market goes in the tank, you reduce the amount you withdraw from your portfolio.

If the market does really well, you can choose to increase the amount you withdraw from your portfolio.

It is a simple concept but building a flexible spending plan has a lot of intricacies and takes careful planning. If you are in the fortunate position to be wondering how you will live off the wealth you have accumulated, this is the case where the advice of a fee-only fiduciary

85 Flexible Spending Rules To Avoid FIREing At 4%. (2019, July 17). https://www.kitces.com/blog/the-problem-with-fireing-at-4-and-the-need-for-flexible-spending-rules/

retirement planner can be extremely valuable in helping to build and execute a flexible spending plan.

It also pays to have flexible income in retirement.

Retirement does not mean you have to stop doing any kind of paid work. Having the *option* to stop doing work of any kind is what matters most. Many will choose to work on a part-time basis doing work they enjoy or pursuing a passion project or business in retirement. Every dollar you earn outside of your portfolio is a dollar you don't have to withdraw from your portfolio.

If you still have a little bit of human capital left after you stop working full-time, it can go a long way in minimizing your sequence of return and longevity risks.

Remember: building wealth requires you to take on investment risk. Living off wealth requires you to manage investment risk.

Chapter 43: 4 Irrational Arguments Against Investing in Index Funds

The evidence presented in this book has painted a clear road map for the rational investor. Invest in low-cost index funds that buy the entire stock market, and basically forget about your portfolio until retirement.

Unfortunately, most investing resources you will come across will not take the rational approach. An entire media and online ecosystem have sprung up to use narratives and guruism to convince investors to do anything other than buying and holding index funds for 40+ years.

I thought it only fitting that we end our journey with a discussion of four irrational and common anti-indexing narratives you will likely hear.

#1: The market is not efficient, so there are plenty of opportunities for active management to outperform

Market efficiency refers to the theory first put forward by Eugine Fama from the University of Chicago, which states in an efficient market, all publically available information is reflected in the current price of a stock.

No stock market is perfectly efficient, but the stock market is efficient enough that investors are better off assuming it is.

If the market is decidedly inefficient, then we should expect actively managed funds to outperform their benchmark index on a consistent basis.

Luckily we can measure this. As we discussed multiple times throughout this book, Standard & Poor's keeps a "Scorecard" that measures how actively managed investment funds perform compared to the local stock market index.[86] At the time I write this, over the past 10 years: **83% of U.S. fund managers underperformed the S&P 500.**

83% of Wall Street managers who have an army of analysts and research at their disposal and whose entire career is centered around beating the market can't do it. But financial bloggers want you to believe they can teach you how to do it.

Another variation of this argument I still hear all the time is, "*Sure, the U.S. market is fairly efficient, but foreign markets are less efficient, and that provides an opportunity for active managers to outperform.*"

Luckily we have that scorecard too.

- 83% of Canadian funds underperformed the TSX
- 85% of European funds underperformed the S&P Europe 350
- 84% of Australian funds underperformed the S&P/ASX 200
- 84% of Japanese funds underperformed the S&P/ASX 200

This narrative is right about one thing: these fund managers have all the opportunity in the world to outperform, and they consistently fail to do so.

#2: Index funds own all the "losers"

Yes, a lot of companies that an index investor owns are underperforming companies.

86 SPIVA | S&P Dow Jones Indices. (n.d.). Www.spglobal.com. https://www.spglobal.com/spdji/en/research-insights/spiva/

Active funds hold plenty of losers, too, as many actively managed funds are little more than "*closet index funds*". These are funds that charge high investment fees but more or less track the market in a similar fashion to index funds.

More to the point, it does not matter if an investment fund holds "the losers". As we covered in Chapter 11, the only way to guarantee success as an investor is to hold "the winners", the 4% of stocks that are responsible for 100% of the gains in the (U.S) stock market since 1926.

The only way to guarantee that you own the future winners is to own everything all the time. 83% of underperforming active fund managers think they can select the winners in advance, but they do not have a crystal ball.

#3: Index funds don't protect your "downside"

This is factually correct.

Index funds do not protect your "downside". If the stock market goes down 40% and you own the entire stock market, your portfolio is also going down 40%—assuming you are 100% invested in stocks. Which, for most people, does not make sense.

This is why we diversify by geography (owning domestic and foreign equity index funds) and by asset class (mainly bonds.)

Active managers try and cushion against a crash by holding a certain percentage of the portfolio in cash. But here's the thing, there's nothing stopping an investor from holding cash in a savings account and receiving some interest rather than paying a Wall Street manager 2% per year to sit on cash.

When active funds hold cash, they underperform in years when the stock market goes up, which is most years.

The data is pretty mixed on whether active mutual funds provide any type of downside protection from a market crash.

A 2020 paper written by Lubos Pastor and Blair Vorsatz titled "Mutual Fund Performance & Fund Flows During the COVID-19 Crisis" found that the majority of active fund managers underperformed their benchmark index during the market crash of 2020.[87]

Active managers failed to "protect the downside" when it mattered most.

You might say, "*How could anyone have seen something like COVID-19 coming ahead of time?*" That might be the single best endorsement of index funds I could think of.

Rational, long-term investors must simply accept that not every year is going to be amazing in the stock market.

#4: You get what you pay for. Low fees = low quality

This is a narrative often put forward by financial advisors whose clients have educated themselves and fire the advisor to self-manage a simple portfolio of index funds.

This is the funniest and most self-serving argument against index funds.

What makes it funny is that it is the exact opposite of the truth. Research from Morningstar found that investment fees are the number

87 Pastor, L., & Vorsatz, M. B. (2020, July 1). Mutual Fund Performance and Flows During the COVID-19 Crisis. National Bureau of Economic Research. https://www.nber.org/papers/w27551

one predictor of future performance.[88] The lower the fees, the higher the expected return for investors.

A more accurate statement would be that active fund investors "don't *get what they pay for*".

What makes this argument self-serving is that when a financial advisor uses a line like this to try and retain a client, it's purely to the benefit of the advisor and often to the detriment of the investor/client.

There is evidence that financial advisors believe in the high-cost mutual funds they are paid to sell.

A 2018 paper written by Linnainmaa et al. titled "The Misguided Beliefs of Financial Advisors" found that most financial advisors sampled in Canada invest their own money in the same way they invest their client's money.[89]

Which is to say, they invest irrationally.

- Chasing past returns
- Investing in high-fee funds
- Under diversifying

Here's the key finding from the paper: "Advisors' ***net returns of −3% per year are similar to their clients' net returns.***"

88 Kinnel, R. (n.d.). How Fund Fees are the Best Predictor of Returns. Morningstar UK. Retrieved June 8, 2022, from https://www.morningstar.co.uk/uk/news/149421/how-fund-fees-are-the-best-predictor-of-returns.aspx

89 Linnainmaa, J. T., Melzer, B., & Previtero, A. (2018, May 16). The Misguided Beliefs of Financial Advisors. Papers.ssrn.com. https://papers.ssrn.com/sol3/papers.cfm?abstract_id=3101426

They also found that the advisors who invest this way continue to do so after they leave the industry, indicating this is more than a show for clients but that they actually believe this is the rational way to invest.

The rational approach is clear

No investment strategy is perfect, and future returns of the stock market are not guaranteed.

The best we can do is invest based on the best available evidence. The evidence is quite clear: the rational approach to investing is to buy and hand full of low-cost index funds, diversify by geography and asset class and hold those investments for several decades regardless of what narrative is dominating the financial news cycle.

ONE LAST THING...

Thank you so much for reading this book. I poured a lot of sweat and tears into it.

Could you do me a favor? Please review this book on Amazon. Whether you thought it was great, terrible, or anywhere in between, I'd love to have your feedback.

Reviews are the best way for an author like me to get discovered. Readers like you can help make it happen.

Thanks in advance,

Ben